"... a must-read for any marketer trying to operate and gain relevancy in today's environment of infinite media, where the consumer not only has a wider span of control but in some cases, with user-generated content, is actually not just our customer but our competition! Change is going to continue to take place. Let's make sure we see it coming and are prepared to respond and engage."

—**LISA BOWMAN,** Executive Vice President and CMO,
United Way Worldwide

"If you're looking for a book with conversion-rate charts, lead funnels, and ROI tables, this isn't it. Sweezey gets back to what we should have been focusing on all along: human behavior, why consumers make the decisions they do, and why context matters more than ever."

—**GEOFFREY COLON,** Head of Brand Studio, Microsoft Advertising;
author, *Disruptive Marketing*

"Thoughtful, up-to-date, and practical insight on how marketing really works today."

—**SETH GODIN,** author, *This Is Marketing*

"A wonderfully helpful, interesting, and thoughtful book that helps place change in the context of the past. All too many books on marketing are hyperbolic, farfetched, or academic. This is a superb book that cuts to the chase of the change that matters and gives you smart practical advice on what to do about it."

—**TOM GOODWIN,** author, *Digital Darwinism*;
Futures Lead, Publicis Groupe

"Whoa. This book is big and broad and deep and smart as hell. It's a comprehensive analysis of how people buy in the Age of Infinite Media and presents a systematic framework to help every marketer rise to the many challenges of change. Read it and put it to work."

—**DOUG KESSLER,** cofounder, Velocity Partners

"Sweezey provides a detailed playbook on how to do Modern Marketing, everything from how brand and advertising must change in the digital era to the deep integration of technology and data to enable you to scale. Buy a copy for every member of your marketing team to transform your relationship with customers."

—**CHARLENE LI,** founder and Senior Analyst,
Altimeter, a Prophet Company; *New York Times*
bestselling author, *The Disruption Mindset*

"With *The Context Marketing Revolution,* Mathew Sweezey provides a road map for how to serve today's media-inundated consumers in the moments that matter. This book should be required reading for A-list brands, B-schools, and C-suites everywhere. It's that fundamental."

—**JEFFREY K. ROHRS,** CMO author, *Audience*

"The new market leaders won't be marketers or brands—they will be customers. Marketers who want to follow their customers' lead need to start with this book."

—**DOC SEARLS,** author, *The Intention Economy*;
coauthor, *The Cluetrain Manifesto*

"If you recognize and accept that marketing has transformed, you are halfway there. This book will help you go the rest of the way by helping you decide what to do about it. Practical advice from a real-world practitioner."

—**DHARMESH SHAH,** cofounder and CTO, HubSpot

THE CONTEXT MARKETING REVOLUTION

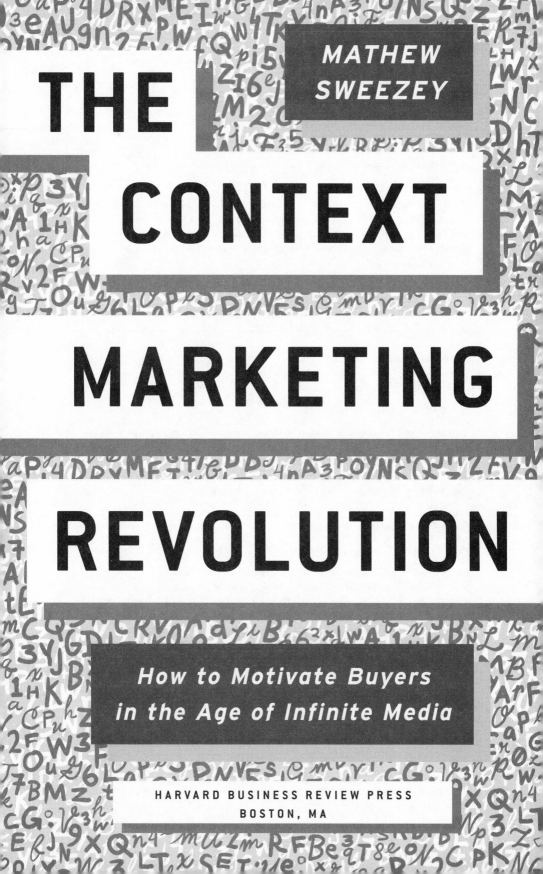

MATHEW
SWEEZEY

THE
CONTEXT
MARKETING
REVOLUTION

*How to Motivate Buyers
in the Age of Infinite Media*

HARVARD BUSINESS REVIEW PRESS
BOSTON, MA

Library of Congress Cataloging-in-Publication Data

Names: Sweezey, Mathew, author. Title: The context marketing revolution :
    how to motivate buyers in the age of infinite media / Mathew Sweezey.
Description: Boston, MA : Harvard Business Review Press, [2019] | Includes index. |
Identifiers: LCCN 2019041090 (print) | LCCN 2019041091 (ebook) |
    ISBN 9781633694026 (hardcover) | ISBN 9781633694033 (ebook)
Subjects: LCSH: Consumers' preferences. | Context effects (Psychology) |
    Market segmentation. | Branding (Marketing)
Classification: LCC HF5415.32 .S85 2020 (print) | LCC HF5415.32 (ebook) |
    DDC 658.8/343—dc23
LC record available at https://lccn.loc.gov/2019041090
LC ebook record available at https://lccn.loc.gov/2019041091

The paper used in this publication meets the requirements of the American National Standard for Permanence of Paper for Publications and Documents in Libraries and Archives Z39.48-1992.

ISBN: 978-1-63369-402-6
eISBN: 978-1-63369-403-3

This book is dedicated to my loving parents,
Ellen Bryson and Frank Sweezey.

Contents

Introduction

Why Context Is King

One morning back in 2014, I felt the familiar buzz from the phone in my pocket. It was a Facebook notification from my friend Cliff, who'd tagged me in a comment on the latest article from *Forbes*. Salesforce, the company I work for, had just been named "Most Innovative Company" in the world for the fourth straight year. But as I settled in to read the story, I felt puzzled. The article, clearly relevant, hadn't reached me that day. I simply had not seen it. What I saw was Cliff's notification, alerting me to the story.

Make no mistake: *Forbes* knows a thing or two about the power of customer experience and modern marketing. And it had many ways to get my attention. It's a publication I write for, and I follow it online. It was pushing media to me daily through my email and Twitter accounts. But while that story would have reached me directly just a few years before, in 2014 it didn't, because by then I was fielding thousands of pieces of media each day. *Forbes*'s emails were getting auto-filed into the abyss of my "unread" tab in Gmail—the catch-all for emails that don't come from colleagues or my direct connections. Similarly, because I was getting thousands of tweets by then, only a tiny fraction ever made it into my Twitter feed.

Despite all my connections to *Forbes*, the media environment had effectively silenced the company's marketing. The success of that article breaking through had nothing to do with the might of *Forbes*'s century-old media powerhouse—and everything to do with my friend Cliff tagging me. "Push" and whatever else the magazine was doing to market and promote itself was no longer enough.

Now I understand why: marketing as we know it had already died.

The Day Consumers Stopped Listening

It happened on June 24, 2009. The death of an era, hidden amid the noise of a political bathroom scandal and the introduction of the iPhone, was silent and invisible. There were no bells, no alarms, no protest. No one even noticed. The day felt just like the one before and the one after it. And yet that moment in June 2009 marked an unprecedented shift in the history of media, business, and I would argue humankind. It was the day when *private individuals*—not brands, not businesses or traditional media outlets—became *the largest producers of media in the world*.

Had we understood the signs, we could have seen it coming. The plight of newspapers and other print media certainly was a harbinger, as was the power of individuals collectively creating political protests using social media, such as during the Arab Spring and Occupy movements. What's more, marketing engagement rates across all media channels had been steadily decreasing while media usage continued to climb.

Clearly a massive change was underfoot, yet none of us realized to what extent. So June 24, 2009, came and went without fanfare. It would take another *eight years* for anyone to realize what had happened. It wasn't until 2017, while researching the future costs of marketing, that I stumbled onto what had occurred back in 2009. I wasn't looking for it—I was merely trying to track the volume of noise and calculate the cost of breaking through in the future.

What I uncovered wasn't just that we had more noise, created mostly by individuals rather than businesses. We had entered into a *new media era*. As I will show in this book, noise is no longer what it once was. More isn't just more—it is exponentially different.

And yet today, judging by how few companies have altered the way they attempt to motivate customers, it's as if that momentous June day never even occurred. My research shows that we marketers continue to stumble around, trying to get customers' attention but succeeding only in annoying them with endless intrusions (think: ads in YouTube videos, telemarketers, and auto-playing videos you must hide before reading an article). If consumers aren't annoyed, it's because they're ignoring advertisers' extraordinarily costly efforts by blocking ads, and increasingly the channels themselves are doing it for them. That's the crazy part: more and more, consumers don't have to lift a finger to avoid you. The environment itself is filtering out brands' attention-seeking messages with the kind of email and social media filters that hid the *Forbes* article from me.

The message couldn't be more obvious: consumers simply aren't listening anymore. They don't have to. Today they're the ones in charge, not marketers. Even though no one noticed, much less acted on, that day in June 2009, it was a tipping point with monumental consequences. It forever redefined how we build relationships, how we connect to the world around us, and even how our economy functions. It ushered in what I call the infinite media era.

Infinite media doesn't mean just more media. It means a radically different *media environment* in which the possibilities are quite literally infinite. What does all this signify for organizations and for marketers in particular? Such a drastic departure from how things once worked can't be met with business as usual. It demands not just new marketing ideas but rather a whole new idea of marketing. It requires a revolution in what we do, how we do it, and the way we think about building brands and motivating customers. No matter what your business's size or type, or what level and kind of job you're in, prepare to embark on a mind-bending way of seeing, selling, and growing your brand, defined by a different kind of marketing in a changed environment.

I call it the *context marketing revolution*. Motivating consumers today has nothing to do with getting their attention and everything to do with their understanding their *context*—that is, their current position in time and space and whatever their task may be in that moment. Today, helping people achieve their immediate goals is the only way to break through the noise and motivate consumers to act.

The era of infinite media has already been unfolding for a decade or more, so we'd better get started. This book will help.

This Changes Everything

Because the way consumers move in the infinite media era is wholly different, brands need to interact with individuals in a wholly different way. Let's step back and look at what came before—call it the limited media era. Beginning in 1900 until about 1995, media creation and distribution were limited to people with the capital to participate—"ad men," agencies, media outlets—so the volume of noise was relatively low and made of a different substance than we have today, as I'll describe later. Since only brands and traditional media outlets could create and distribute noise, they were solely competing with each other, using creative messaging to steal people's attention and push their wares. Sex sold, and brands used subliminal tricks to become "top of mind." Publication and promotion were the backbone of building a brand.

With the rise of consumer email use in the 1990s, we saw the first glimpse of the revolution.[1] As time progressed, more and more consumers were *becoming* the media—creating, tweeting, posting, and sharing—until that fateful day in June 2009 when the scales tipped. With the beginning of the infinite media era, the shift to a new master, the individual, was complete. Businesses were no longer in charge of the media environment. Their monopoly had ended.

In coming chapters, we'll explore in depth what the differences between the limited and infinite eras mean. But for now it's enough to understand that the new era transformed everything—the very notion of what noise is, what consumers desire, and how brands break through. No longer are those things done in a limited and static way, but rather in a manner that is infinitely dynamic. To win in the infinite media era, we all need to grasp a truth that's both simple and complex. What matters isn't ads, creative messaging, elegant copy, or even dazzling content—what matters is context: understanding how to help consumers achieve their goals in the moment.

The Swedish furniture giant IKEA has mastered this notion of context. But that wasn't always the case. The stories were legendary: frustrated, disillusioned customers attempting to find their way through the massive warehouse and then lugging home their just-purchased bookshelf or table in an enormous flat box—only to come face-to-face with a challenging set of assembly instructions. To improve customer experience and increase sales, IKEA bought the gig-economy startup TaskRabbit. So, starting in 2017, IKEA customers can hire an independent handyperson to pick up, deliver, and assemble that table or shelf by using the TaskRabbit app, in real time, through a process similar to ordering a car with Uber or Lyft. Customers love it, and why wouldn't they? IKEA found a way to meet consumers at their precise point of need, that is, in the context of their current goal to have their furniture delivered and assembled, hassle-free.

IKEA is one company that I, working with a research team at Salesforce, identified as a "high performer." Our criteria were based on a blind survey we issued each year for four years to businesses worldwide of every vertical, size, and geography (a total of eleven thousand businesses).[2] The data points we gathered told us a lot about what marketing tools and tactics worked well for those anonymous companies. Specifically, we found that the companies that enjoyed consistent growth were those that stayed focused on *crafting experiences across the customer journey.*[3] The data showed that those companies—only 16 percent of the thousands of companies surveyed—were almost ten times more likely than the others to register significant, consistent wins over their direct competition. That means that the future of the other 84 percent of the companies in our survey depends on their ability to follow in the footsteps of that top 16 percent.

Next, we used the criteria from those top-growth companies in the blind survey to look for companies and brands that seemed to follow those same practices. Besides IKEA, we uncovered other high performers, such as Tesla, Room & Board, Oreo, Airbnb, and WeWork, all of which seemed to understand the notion of context and what's needed to navigate consistently in the infinite media era. That is, all of our high performers had adopted a new idea of marketing—not just new marketing ideas.

The Changes Keep Coming

Before we continue, keep in mind an important truth about the future, given the speed at which things are moving and the magnitude of the metamorphosis. Today I'm telling you that individuals, not brands, are in charge. But the reason we have to get context marketing right is because things are rapidly changing still: our individual devices and apps have become the second-largest creators of media. And it isn't just more media; rather, it's extremely powerful media, able to motivate consumers unlike anything before.

All of which is to say that artificial intelligence (AI) is already here. The AI in our devices continually reminds or alerts us—and we've changed our behavior in response. Think of the Fitbit and its power to get you to take five hundred more steps to reach your daily goal. Don't want to be late? Your calendar will notify you thirty minutes before your appointment and again fifteen minutes later. Want to be more mindful, lose weight, learn a language? Get an app or device to be your personal assistant. It can read your personal data feed, alerting you to exactly what to do and when. Each app and device becomes a personal media stream created just for you, sent just to you at the correct moment, motivating you in novel ways. That's what I mean by the importance of context to our transformed environment.

The fact is, we can't do without AI in the era of infinite media. The massive content glut from brands, individuals, and devices has made AI indispensable. AI curates our inboxes, Google search queries, websites, apps, and social feeds. Consumers see only what AI selects for them to see (and eventually, AI will also be the major creator of that content). Again, everything is contextual, and AI's importance as the controller only increases as we move forward in time and noise rises even higher. Context isn't just what consumers want; it's what AI optimizes for. That is why context is the key and AI the barrier we must break through to reach and motivate the modern consumer. More on all of this later in the book. For now, understand that the context marketing revolution is crucial—not only for today but also for a future in which AI curates or creates most of the content we see.

The Context Marketing Revolution—and a New Model for Growth

Because the foundation on which marketing traditionally stood has flipped and multiplied across infinitely larger territory, we marketers find ourselves standing on new ground, with brand-new rules. It took us all this time to realize it, but make no mistake: starting on June 24, 2009, everything that once worked in marketing, stopped. *What* we do, *how* we do it, and *who* does it were transformed forever.

Fortunately, we have some guidelines: our research into today's high-performing marketing organizations reveals a way to navigate this shifting ground, no matter how large your business or what kind, whether you're a leader at a company or agency, or a member of a marketing team. The change needed, however, isn't simply another iteration of what you've done before. Context marketing requires a recrafted lens to view how the whole landscape has shifted in three key aspects:

- **What We Do.** In today's era of infinite media, marketing must move from attention-getting schemes (which today's consumers filter out) to working within the contexts in which people find themselves. As the example of IKEA illustrates, the *scope* of marketing must refocus to work within a diverse and infinite set of contexts to help consumers achieve their immediate goals.

- **How We Do It.** Today, marketers can't just broadcast static messages; rather, they need to create and provide dynamic experiences. Tesla is a master at crafting the kinds of experiences that engage consumers, as I'll describe shortly. Businesses everywhere must follow Tesla's example and rethink their *execution* of marketing: marketers must become engineers of perpetual systems where scale is achieved through agility and automation, not broader reach. The level of personal engagement required to achieve the expanded levels of context simply cannot be reached otherwise. Ad campaigns give way to holistic systems, such as automated customer journeys, artificially intelligent websites, and predictive and proactive customer support.

- **Who Does It.** Individuals, not businesses or brands, are now the chief noise makers. That means executive leadership must reenvision the *role* of marketing to motivate consumers and drive growth. In this new businesses model, marketing has an expanded role and multiple levers to increase revenue far past net new sales. For example, Salesforce marketing created a customer-community site called Trailblazer, where customers engage with each other and with the company. As a result, buyers associated with this largely community-run site spend twice as much money on Salesforce services and stay on as customers four times as long as do non-Trailblazer-community customers. In other words, Salesforce has dramatically increased its profitablity—without ever creating a new customer.

As this book will show, those three shifts in marketing's scope, execution, and role demand a revised growth model that brands must follow. Where once we clung to the idea of *build-market-sell*, brands will survive only with a formulation of that model that's been flipped and expanded: *market-sell-build-market*. I call this new model the context marketing model, and I'll describe it in detail later in this introduction.

Right about now you might be thinking that this doesn't really sound so new, that you've heard some of these ideas before. And you have, at least in part. The problem is what companies have done with those ideas and the gaps that remain. We'll need to bridge those gaps before we can begin to meet the demands of the infinite media era.

Everything New Is New Again

The need for change has not been lost on brands. Companies and marketing organizations have tried to improve and expand their mediums, formats, and channels. The trouble is that they've left the foundational ideas of marketing alone. We're all versed on the consumer's desire for experiences, as laid out back in 1999 by Joseph Pine and James Gilmore in their breakout book, *The Experience Economy*. The authors empirically proved that experiences that help consumers transform ultimately create the highest value for businesses. But rather than gaining a deep understanding of the authors' notion of experience as a system of connected moments, most brands simply recast old ideas. They took their static ads and made them immersive, and they made their physical products digital—all while using the same old ideas, businesses models, and marketing methods.

The same year that Pine and Gilmore's book appeared, we learned about the power of permissioned media to directly reach audiences as foretold by Seth Godin's *Permission Marketing*. And again brands leapt to adopt "permissioned" methods for email but ignored the important foundation the book describes: value exchange. Consumers will give you the data, permission, and access to the most personal parts of their lives as long as you use those things to deliver the value they seek. That value also shifts with time. When Godin crafted his masterpiece, content was limited, so consumers valued brands sending them content. Now content is infinite, and consumers value experiences. *Forbes* had permission to reach me, and it didn't matter. My inbox filtered the magazine's email into the "unimportant" folder, burying it under hundreds of others, while my social channels filtered out the *Forbes* notification completely. Consumers do not want mass experiences; they desire personal moments. The requirement of asking for permission has not changed—how we use it has. It has morphed into something greater: it is the key that marketers need to gain access to your inbox and the data we need in order to create personal experiences, not just improve mass messages.

The notion of value exchange that Godin wrote about applies to many other recent marketing ideas as well, such as content marketing (brands creating their own content to engage their audiences) and inbound marketing (brands designing content that specifically answers people's search-engine questions and then directs them to the brand's own site). Both ideas are correct, yet most brands fail to understand why they work or what consumers value about them. No consumer ever said, "I want content." Content is only an intermediary to achieve a goal at a specific moment—to answer people's questions, to entertain them, to validate their identity. Those are specific *experiences* that people desire, not "content." In other words, without a new idea of marketing that is built on the notion of using permission to create value that consumers desire in the moment, it doesn't matter what methods you apply. They are dead on arrival.

Along with their versions of experience, permission, and content, brands more recently have adopted more systematic pathways of growth, as laid out a few years ago in such books as *Hacking Growth* by Sean Ellis and Morgan Brown and *From Impossible to Inevitable* by Aaron Ross and Jason Lemkin. But again, if brands undertake these efforts without a contextual lens, they will fail. Not because the ideas in any of those books aren't correct, but rather because brands are using them as simple tweaks on their same old ideas. That is not what these authors were suggesting, yet it is what most brands have done, and then they wonder why nothing's really improved in their ability to motivate customers.

The truth most brands haven't recognized is that their old *ideas* of marketing—the ones on which brands have been pinning new faces (like experiences, permission, content, and different paths to growth)—are the problem. That is why that day in June 2009, when the switch flipped and the infinite media era dawned, is so critical. It's the hard evidence showing why those ideas once worked, why they failed, and what we need to do about it.

In fact, given just how drastically the world upended in 2009, we might well wonder how marketers everywhere missed it—me included, at least for a while.

Why Marketing Missed the Memo

Perhaps we marketers were simply racing too hard while running in the wrong direction. Over the past decade or more, we diligently and creatively adopted new channels, changed our messaging, tailored our brand voice, and increased our product's value to customers in every way imaginable. We've allocated and reallocated digital spend to connect with prospects on their journey, to win them and retain them. To accomplish all of that, we've forged better working relationships with IT and sales, working together to design apps, to relaunch websites, and to build landing pages for campaigns that ooze with data.

Each of those efforts, when they were first adopted, did move the needle. But too many brands didn't understand *why* their efforts worked, so today they are floundering. What they needed to understand were things like the following: Apps work when they are the best way to accomplish a task, not because consumers desire apps. Permission works because it gives the individual control, not because it gets brands' marketing emails through. Content and inbound marketing work because they let consumers make up their own minds.

But there are other reasons we marketers are falling short. We are still relying on marketing commandments that are fossils of a bygone era. Ideas like "sex sells," or keeping your brand "top of mind" for consumers, or "there's no such thing as bad press" are notions the infinite media era has made obsolete. Images that flash skin or smoldering looks just don't sell as they once did because consumers aren't even looking at ads—and if they do, they're unlikely to remember brand names because people now operate in a completely different world.

The changed media environment has spawned a brand-new kind of consumer, one who transcends defined categories such as age demographics and business-to-business (B2B) versus business-to-consumer (B2C). And that new consumer has developed novel ways for remembering things and fresh processes for making decisions, amounting to an entirely altered customer journey, as I'll describe in more detail in chapter 1. We marketers have accounted for none of these shifts, perhaps in part because our own company leaders have mostly been blind to how much the transformed media environment has changed the ways we do business.

Indeed, digital-age leaders have reexamined and redefined just about every aspect of their business model *except* marketing. They see the vast expansion of media as simply the multiplication of channels, with free distribution and better ad targeting, not a whole new business environment. And in that limited view, they fail to understand this current environment's profound effect on consumers' behavior and motivation. More significantly, they fail to understand its effect on their business: how it has fundamentally altered how they should create value for consumers and establish long-term relationships with them.

The point is that, whether any of us realized it or not, June 24, 2009, marked the day that consumers completed the transition into an altogether changed environment. This created fresh possibilities and a seismic shift in buyer behaviors and values. Brands that fail to grasp that truth will never break through, just as *Forbes* didn't break through to me with a relevant news story about my company.

Unfortunately, all signs point to one indisputable fact: *almost no one* has grasped the truth of the infinite media era. Marketers continue doing the same old things as if nothing is different. Again, it's not working. This becomes clear in a survey conducted by Forrester Research in 2018. The survey found that B2B marketers with a managed lead flow converted only 1.15 percent of every one hundred leads they generated into a sale. Which means those marketers' idea of marketing fails 98.85 percent of the time to generate revenue.[4]

Moreover, consumers have shown us they don't even *like* advertising, and they've had enough: six hundred million devices today use ad blocking software. Such mass consumer action to filter out marketing is "easily the largest boycott in the history of the world," as Doc Searls, Harvard fellow and coauthor of *The Cluetrain Manifesto*, reminded me in a recent conversation. Simply put, the consumer is in charge, not marketers like you and me.

Not only do people dislike advertising, but they also don't trust it or the people creating it. The 2018 Gallup poll of the most trusted professions found advertising professionals as the fourth-least-trusted profession, preceded only by members of Congress (#1), car salespeople (#2), and telemarketers (#3).[5] Lawyers are now more trusted than advertising professionals. This data should be smacking us in the face. Advertisers, marketers, and salespeople—the very professions we've created to grow our businesses—have become the most distrusted professions in America.

The hard truth is that consumers have always distrusted advertising, almost as much as they dislike being "sold to." But in the limited era, they didn't have any recourse. Today, not only do they have powerful recourse to bypass marketing, but the infinite environment is doing it *for* them through all the ways people now connect, engage, and share.

Think of the difference between a YouTube ad campaign, which you want to skip (but can't), and an offer of the TaskRabbit app from IKEA to get the help you need to assemble your newly bought table in record time. The former is undesirable and nonpermissioned; the latter is hugely desirable and highly permissioned, and consumers will pay for it. To succeed as marketers in this modern era, we must focus on providing experiences that are desired and permissioned wherever possible. In other words, contextual experiences.

The Way Forward

One very important aspect of this revolution in the way the new media works is that neither consumers nor marketers control it. The media environment is (and forever will be) driven by algorithms. As the level of noise has risen, algorithms have played an increasing role in helping consumers make sense of the modern world, and we are now at a point of no return. The amount of noise is far past human cognition, and AI is a native aspect of every modern interaction—behind the screens, ensuring that individuals get exactly what they want, when they want it. In other words, consumers have adopted a novel decision-making process (which we will begin to explore in chapter 2), shaped by their intense daily relationship with today's media environment.

The result is that now people can be exposed to an experience, and become engaged with it, only when it's contextual—that is, when it algorithmically appears on their new (extraordinarily personal) customer journey. A brand experience that is the most contextual in the moment stands the highest chance of playing the algorithm game correctly, reaching consumers, and driving the growth that businesses seek.

How do we make that happen? Our study of high performers in the infinite media era reveals a clear path, one that takes into account today's consumer psychology. To craft contextual brand moments that will break through and drive engagement, marketers must ensure experiences that are (1) available, (2) permissioned, (3) personal, (4) authentic, and (5) purposeful. Those are the five elements of context, and they are so crucial to getting context marketing right that we will spend all of part two learning about them.

But there's more. Motivating consumers in the infinite media era also requires a fresh understanding of how marketing builds brands and drives action. In the limited era, consumer motivation was a by-product of creative campaigns that told people about the products or services that companies created. Brands crafted a single message so compelling that people acted. Today motivation is a by-product of many connected moments, requiring brands to have a systematic effort that is holistic and perpetual. It begins long before a company builds a product or releases a service, and it extends long past the product's or service's use.

That's what I meant earlier when I said the context marketing revolution essentially spawns a recrafted model for consumer motivation and building brands: *market-sell-build-market*, which is the context marketing model (CMM). Think about Tesla, which built its market for the Model 3 long before it began selling or even making the car. As a result, when Model 3 presales became available, it was cited as the biggest one-week launch of any product ever, preselling more than one hundred thousand cars in a matter of hours.[6] Tesla did that by engaging consumers, over a period of time, in a number of experiences that contained all five elements of context that we just listed.

For example, the company's founder, Elon Musk, built a massive *permissioned* audience on social media that was engaged around a central *purpose*: radical innovation to get the world off fossil fuel. Musk's personal Twitter feed is full of rocket launches, discussions about solar panels, tours of Tesla's new production facility (aptly named the Gigafactory), and even a video of him launching a car into space. All of this is *authentic*, as it fits directly in line with the value that the company's audience members expected when they gave permission. They follow both Musk and Tesla for that over-the-top content, experiences that are *available* in the context of the moment. Tesla then used this deep connection to cobuild the car with its audience, asking audience members to fund the production of the Model 3 by preordering. They did.

But the Tesla experience doesn't stop there. Even after the order is placed, the company continues its marketing efforts by providing over-the-top customer experiences. For example, a Tesla team member reaches out in a *personal* way to let each buyer know when his or her car is being made, then follows up to let the buyer choose how the car should be delivered. Finally, team members ask buyers to share their amazing experience with others through an advocacy program where Tesla customers can earn rewards by taking action.

The result? Today Musk's audience on Twitter is seven times that of Tesla's closest competitor, Mercedes-Benz, and the company spends a miniscule amount on advertising (1/150th the amount that Mercedes-Benz spends); yet it sells *three times* as many cars. The impressive part is the sustainability of this model of market-sell-build-market. It was the same model Tesla used to launch all three of its previous cars, and it continues to work. In 2018, two years after Tesla launched the Model 3, it became the best-selling luxury car in the United States.[7]

Tesla isn't alone, as we'll see in the examples of high performers throughout this book. These are brands on a journey with their customers, defined by a novel business model tailor-made for the infinite media era. In part three of this book, I will walk you through each stage of the CMM and illustrate how your brand can craft customer experiences with the winning formula of market-sell-build-market. But there's more. With the context marketing revolution, we're reimagining all aspects of marketing, including the methods we use to produce it. That means finding ways of building automated programs that can manage and optimize massive new networks of customer experiences. Building such programs doesn't take more creativity or even better innovation. Our research at Salesforce found that a particular method—*agile*—enabled the high-performing marketing organizations we studied to focus on crafting the most value per unit of time possible. Part three will cover in detail what agile is and how to use agile, but for now understand that creative ideas are only the start, the hypotheses. Working those ideas through agile methods is what raises them to their highest value.

About this Book

In part one, we strip away outdated ideas of what marketing is "supposed to be" and examine in detail the context marketing revolution and why we need it. Chapter 1 looks closely at the fundamental differences between how we once motivated customers in the limited media era and how we must motivate them in today's infinite media era. What's needed now is context marketing, which entails a shift in marketing's *scope* (what we do), *execution* (how we do it), and *role* (who does it). Chapter 2 describes how the changed media environment has spawned both a new kind of consumer—one who transcends defined categories such as age demographics and B2B versus B2C—and a new consumer decision-making process or journey, which requires a revolution in how marketers approach their brands and customers.

Part two focuses on the five elements of *context* that are key to the context marketing revolution. Chapter 3 provides an overview of context and how its five elements (the context framework) can guide marketers to create the kinds of experiences that are all-important for consumers today, and how those experiences work together to motivate customers in new ways. Then, each of chapters 4–8 examines one of the five elements of context that craft the customer experience. That is, experiences that are *available* (helping people achieve the value they seek in the moment); *permissioned* (coordinating with individuals to give them what they've asked for, on their terms); *personal* (going beyond how personal the experience is, to how personally you can deliver it); *authentic* (combining voice, empathy, and channel congruence simultaneously); and *purposeful* (creating a deeper connection to the brand beyond the product).

In part three I show how to break through the noise to execute context marketing in the infinite era. I provide a revised rulebook that showcases how high performers employ context-based marketing to build modern brands and dominate their marketplaces. Chapter 9 describes how marketers can shift from telegraphing static ad campaigns to crafting perpetually flowing customer journeys. These are journeys that apply across all businesses and sizes and demographics to powerfully reshape the way you grow your brand. The chapter includes specific questions you can ask in customer interviews, which will help you understand your brand's various buyer personas as you begin to map their journeys. Chapter 10 looks at the concept of *triggers*, which are key moments that marketers can engage to connect or reconnect individuals to their customer journeys. The chapter describes two kinds of triggers—natural and targeted—and how to use them to keep consumers moving forward through each stage in a continuous flow of context.

But how do we *scale* such flowing rivers of customer experiences? Chapter 11 describes how contextual marketers must learn to leverage complex systems of data, technology, and automated programs to carry customers through their journeys, stage by stage. Such automation is the only way we can instantly create and execute programs in real time. Even with automations, however, there simply isn't enough time in the day to do it all. That's why we need a revolutionary way of working, which I describe in chapter 12: *agile*. High-performing marketing organizations today such as Twitter, Airbnb, and Facebook have embraced agile—a process of rapid testing of hypotheses—which allows them to produce the highest level of value per unit of time. Embracing agile enables us to move toward an innovative model for doing business, which is the final step of the context marketing revolution, as detailed in chapter 13. That is, contextual marketing leads inevitably to transformed organizational structures and roles that are required to execute the CMM, already being embraced by companies like Tesla. Such a model goes hand in hand with other novel processes needed in the infinite media era, such as a reporting method—the weighted pipeline—that offers a holistic and predictive measure of marketing efforts.

Finally, chapter 14 concludes the book with a call to action that will help marketers take the first step needed to start the revolution: getting executive buy-in. Proving to your top executives that contextual marketing is the only path forward toward growth will be key to its success, and this final chapter offers some insights on how to do that.

Consider this your guidebook for the revolution. Billions of people strong, this revolution is unlike any that's come before. And make no mistake:

membership is not optional; the revolution affects everyone and everything. The context marketing revolution isn't about content, social media, ad blocking, or mobility. It's about what people derive from instant access, connectivity, and openness. It's about a novel set of shared values, desires, and purpose found within the infinite media era that would have been impossible in an earlier time. By its very nature, this revolution is already unlocking deeper levels of humanity, power, and connectivity between individuals. It's a revolution in what consumers demand, how they make decisions, and how brands fulfill those needs.

Let's begin by exploring in detail how and why the infinite media era makes traditional marketing obsolete, and delve into three keys of contextual marketing. The shift from limited media to infinite media changed who the players in marketing are, what we marketers do, and how we do it. That is, it ushered in the context marketing revolution that will powerfully reshape the way you motivate cutomers and grow your brand.

Part One

HOW INFINITE MEDIA HAS TRANSFORMED YOUR BUSINESS FOREVER

1.

Three Keys to the Context Marketing Revolution

Think back to February 2016, and you might remember a change to your Google search results page. Google Ads (formerly called AdWords)—the list of ads that always lined the right-hand margin of your results—had disappeared. The ads began to appear instead at the top (and sometimes bottom) of our search lists, a far less prominent placement. The move was a strange one for a company that makes more than $100 billion each year from advertising sales. But the change sent a clear signal: our new world has no place for old ideas.

Google Ads is the apex of targeted marketing, the perfection of one-to-one, powered by algorithms that run on the mightiest supercomputers available. It accesses the world's largest database of personal information and combines it with real-time search data that defines the user's exact intent. Then it matches that specific data with what it believes is the correct ad for the moment.

So why did Google decide to make the change? The company's stated reasons: decreased engagement rates on those right-hand ads and a wish to provide a more positive consumer experience. Soon after the shift in Google's ad placement, WordStream (a software company that sells tools to brands that help them manage their Google Ads) did some digging. Looking at more than $1 billion ad spend over two years by customers on the WordStream platform, it found that, on average, Google's ads drove consumer action only 1.98 percent of the time.[1] In starker terms, it *failed to drive any action 98.02 percent of the time.* What's more, only 15 percent of those consumer actions were prompted by the right-hand ads. So, despite Google's ads being the perfect message at the perfect time, those right-hand ads drove action in only 0.3 percent of consumers.[2]

Clearly, when the world's most powerful technology company, leveraging more data and computing power than anyone dreamed possible, can't make the apex of marketing theory work, it's time to come up with a new idea of what marketing is. This was inevitable, of course. Print got outplayed by the radio jingles of the 1930s, which got overrun by TV commercials in the 1950s. Banner ads of the 1990s matured into an array of digital ads in the 2000s, and now (sleight of hand!) posts promoted by influencers and other slices of social media are dominating the 2010s. The question marketers ask nearly every day is, where do we need to be? We're constantly chasing new buzzwords and channels, and while the pace is fast, we are generally comfortable riding this trajectory. We don't question what we *do* so much as which channel we use.

The problem is that we've become so comfortable in our individual marketing microcosms (PR, advertising, social media, digital), we failed to notice that the golden age of marketing, and all that made it golden, ended a good number of years ago. Yet we continue relying on long-standing ways of driving business that simply don't perform as they once did, much to the frustration of organizations and leadership. Too many of us have blamed the fast pace of technology. We've all felt everyone else was creating better ads or targeting better or "getting" social media sooner. But in all our striving to be cutting edge, we didn't understand one very important change: the consumer is done listening to us. The consumer is in charge and has been in charge since June 2009 when the infinite media era began. And in case anyone needed reminding, think about those six hundred million devices today using ad-blocking software.

This chapter examines the profound transition we've undergone since the limited media era and why we marketers continue to act as if nothing has changed—to our peril. I also detail the three elements of context marketing and how they can work to bridge the gap between the old and new eras.

But first, let me share with you how this book came into being and the startling research behind it.

Multiple Studies—One Big Discovery

From 2015 through 2019, I worked with a team of researchers at Salesforce to identify the key traits of high-performing marketing organizations around the world. Each year we deployed a blind global survey and examined many thousands of brands from all sectors. Over the four years, we surveyed more than eleven thousand businesses, and through those multiple studies we've been able to pinpoint how the high performers differed from everyone else. We found that both high and low performers used things like social media, content marketing, and inbound marketing. They all read the same books and followed the same people. Yet high-performing marketing organizations were more likely to outperform their direct competitors—significantly, by a *factor of 96.3 times*[3]—compared with the low performers.

What did they do differently? Across every industry, in every geography, all high performers had full executive support and buy-in to a revolutionary change: not new marketing ideas, but *a new idea of marketing*. The Salesforce studies also revealed that high-performing marketing organizations were centrally focused on customer *experiences*. Everything those companies did—their metrics, tactics, roles, and business goals—traced back to the experiences they created.

As I pointed out in the introduction, we all know that the importance of "the customer experience" isn't a new insight. But our analysis showed that the high performers' *definition* of customer experience differs from that of most businesses. It would have to be different, right? If customer experience is known to all business, yet these high performers were more likely beating their direct competition—by a magnitude of almost ten—there must be a difference in their concept of customer experience.

We found that difference to be their grasp of how the new media environment operates, or more specifically, *for whom* it operates. Recall the example with which I began this book—how I missed an important *Forbes* story even though I was on all of the company's marketing and internal lists. It finally did get my attention, amid all the other noise I was dealing with that day, but only because my friend Cliff pinged me about it.

So why was an individual able to break through when a media power-house couldn't? The answer is fairly simple in theory: in this new environ-ment, the consumer reigns. We already understand this to some degree. As I mentioned, our research showed that both high and low performers use similar tactics and channels, such as social media, that all focus on in-dividual needs. Yet the low performers aren't breaking through. As my experience with *Forbes* illustrates, the current media environment effec-tively silenced the company's marketing, despite all my connections with *Forbes*. So, the next piece of the puzzle I needed to understand was our environment.

During the same time as the Salesforce studies, I was conducting sepa-rate research into the future cost of marketing, and specifically how much it would cost to break through the noise. This required me to first trace media backward as far as we can reliably track it (1900) and project for-ward to 2030 using current trajectories. From there I was able to examine the three layers of our media environment: players, noise, and channels. *Players* are those creating and distributing noise. *Noise* is any piece of *noticed* media created and distributed by a player, whether that player is a business, an individual, or a device. By this definition, the thousands of posts that your social networks create (that never make it to your feed), the hundreds of billboards (that you drive by but never look at), and the end-less consumer packaged goods you pass by every day are not accounted for in this study—because if you can't see them or don't take them in, they are unlikely to have any effect. Finally, the last environmental layer of *channel* is any medium where messages can be created, distributed, and consumed. This broad definition allowed me to account for modern aspects of our en-vironment, such as notifications, texts, and messaging applications.

After analyzing a massive amount of data, I found that high performers weren't just better at leveraging technology, quicker to adopt new channels, or more creative. Rather, they were playing a whole new game designed for a changed media environment. What those companies intrinsically knew, the data confirmed: one era of media had ended and another had begun—and

June 24, 2009, when individuals began to dominate media creation, was the tipping point.

Limited Gives Way to the Infinite

During the limited media era (1900–1995), as the name implies, media creation and distribution were limited to those that had the required capital to participate—predominantly businesses—and channels distributed whatever messages that dominant group promoted. Those constraints meant the total volume of noise was relatively low. This era gave birth to the golden age of marketing (1955–1970), the rise of mega advertising agencies, and the huge emphasis on branding. Marketers delivered one message at a time, and it was the same for everyone.

When email first emerged in 1971, it was an underground network used by only a few hundred people. It didn't really begin to reach larger adoption until the 1990s, when networked personal computers and mail clients opened the medium up to the masses.[4] From there things began to change as more and more consumers got connected and started creating, tweeting, posting, and sharing media until, as described in the introduction, the scales tipped on one particular day in June 2009. On that day, the data clearly shows that private individuals overtook businesses to become the largest and most powerful creators of media. From that point forward, business was no longer master of the media environment, and all channels began to optimize for the individual media creators. The monopoly that brands and organizations had held for more than a century no longer held sway.

Significantly, the concept of marketing—the one the majority of us still use—was created and iterated many times throughout the limited media era. But it wasn't until that June day in 2009 that the underlying *foundation* of our media environment shifted. Hints of the groundswell escaped the notice of most of us, such as how individuals on social media were creating massive global protests. Despite profound changes in how people were using social and mobile media, it didn't occur to many of us that our long-standing ideas about marketing would so quickly become obsolete.

It's now clear that modern media hasn't simply multiplied; it is a radically different environment on a macro scale, completely attuned to a new goal. Rather than delivering one message at a time—the same message—to everyone (billboard style), the infinite media era uses algorithms to connect the right people to the right content in real time.

That is why marketing stopped working and why today's high-performing marketing organizations seem to understand something that lower performers don't. Specifically, the infinite media era reversed or replaced three foundational characteristics of the limited media era—the who, what, and how of motivating consumers.

Those three aspects also imply the way forward: the changes marketers must make in the context marketing revolution.

Three Keys to Context Marketing

First, the shift from the limited to the infinite era recasts *who* the actors (or players) are. *Individuals replace businesses as the dominant creators of noise*, so that today consumers make *three times* the noise of all businesses combined. And it's not just more; it is a new type of noise that engages consumers for different, more compelling reasons, as described in the next shift.

Second, the shift to the infinite media era changes *what* we do (or to put it another way, it changes the kind of noise we make). *Context replaces attention as marketing's modus operandi.* In the limited media era, marketing used attention-seeking methods to distract individuals *away* from the task at hand in order to sell messages; in the era of infinite media, context seeks to match a brand *with* the task at hand by creating an experience that fulfills each consumer's desire in the moment, which brings us to the third shift.

Third, the infinite media era changes *how* (or the channel through which) messages are best conveyed. *Static messages give way to dynamic experiences.* The infinite era media environment is focused on individuals, and they value experiences. Marketers must shift from being the creators of messages to acting as the owners and sustainers of all brand experiences, which are served up only *when and where individuals want them.* This is what the high-performing marketing organizations from our study prove is radically more effective than trying to get people's attention with messaging campaigns.

Let's look at each of those three shifts more closely and what they imply about how to reach today's consumers.

Noise Makers Aren't Who They Used to Be

In 2018, more people on our planet had a mobile device (7.3 billion[5]) than had electricity (6.7 billion[6]). And the majority of those 7 billion devices allowed people to create, distribute, and access as much content as they desired.

Think about it: now is the first time in the history of the world that such a level of media exchange and consumption has been possible, and practically frictionless at that. Increasingly, our devices themselves are creating content: research by IHS Markit estimates that by 2025, there will be fifteen connected devices per person on the planet, each one capable of consuming, creating, and distributing media, without human aid.[7] Thus, our current infinite media era is living up to its name, with no end in sight to the domination of individuals and their devices or the increasing amount of content they will create.

So it comes as no surprise that noise is more than one hundred times greater than it was when first measured in 1900, but that doesn't account for the fact that noise is also much more complicated. If we call everything noise, we are lumping together very different kinds and assuming that they all function similarly. That's not the case. In the limited era, media was dominated by noise from businesses, mostly advertisements and marketing messages; the infinite era introduced individual noise, such as texts, social posts, emails, and other device noise, such as app notifications. The sheer variety and volume of noise mean people must be more selective about what noise they let in.

All noise today, however, can generally be broken down into one of two categories: noise generated by businesses and noise generated by individuals (and their individual devices). When we view noise through those two

FIGURE 1-1

Business noise vs. individual noise, 1900–2030 (projected)

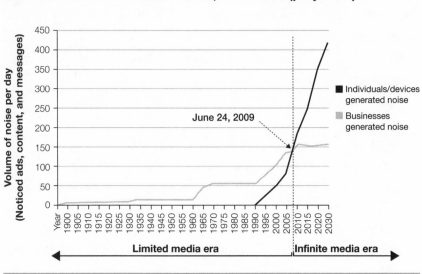

lenses, we get a much clearer picture of why we need a revolution in our idea of marketing to break through it.

Let's first consider business noise: print ads, radio commercials, TV ads, email campaigns, sponsored social posts, and the like. In figure 1-1, note the spike in the total volume of business-generated noise after the introduction of each new major channel: radio (1920), television (1940), and finally, the internet (1990) and social media (2000). Each spike is followed by a ceiling—a saturation point, if you will—beyond which business noise cannot grow until another media channel enters the environment. The important takeaway here is that business noise is a by-product of *market opportunity*, not of consumer desire.

In contrast, noise created by individuals and devices has a much different growth pattern, with no saturation points. That noise—tweets, posts, texts, notifications, and videos, to name just a few—begins with the mass consumer use of email in the 1990s and continues to climb at a relatively astounding rate. As the figure makes clear, in 2009 the volume of individual noise surpassed the volume of business noise and never turned back.

After years of increasing levels of individual noise, the average consumer in 2018 noticed 500 pieces of noise per day: 150 of those were created by businesses, which were dwarfed by 350 pieces from individuals. Two things stand out in this growth pattern. First, individual noise is not just steadily growing; it doesn't seem to have a saturation point, and that's for one profound reason: it is desired (permissioned) by the individual. Second, because permissioned noise is highly valued, it is very likely to persuade and motivate individuals, much more than the unwanted business noise ever could.

Noise, therefore, is very different from what it used to be. So how can a business (i.e., marketing) break through? It must act more like individual noise.

Noise Isn't What *It Once Was*

The second shift that occurred between the limited media era and today's era of infinite media was a dramatic change in the very nature of noise. Noise used to be anything that brands and businesses could put out there that would catch the consumer's attention, no matter what he or she was in the middle of doing. The louder, shinier, brighter, and bigger—the better.

The infinite media era has changed all that: attention has been replaced by context. In other words, the algorithm of any given channel—be it a Google search, Amazon search, Apple News, email, Facebook news feed, or some other digital media—will select a media experience only when the channel determines that the experience offers enough *context* to drive an individual's engagement. Further, that individual will engage only if and when the media experience meets his or her need within the immediate context of that moment.

Perhaps the best way to prove the significance of context—and the vast difference between the limited media era and our current infinite one—is to look at how many of our long-held basic truisms about marketing no longer work.

Four "Attention-Getting Rules" of a Bygone Era

Let's start with the one that practically everyone knows: sex sells. It was the limited era's ultimate attention-grabber. Skin, compromising positions, smoldering looks. According to *Ad Age*, in March 2017 the agency 72and-Sunny announced that its newest campaign for Carl's Jr. and Hardee's was an express effort to be known for "food, not boobs," and to move the brands past years of marketing that featured bikini babes.[8] As Jason Norcross, executive creative director for Carl's Jr., explained, "Those ads just weren't driving business as they once did."

It may have been pure luck that those ads ever worked at all. A study by the University of Illinois tracked eighty years of advertising data and found that "people remember ads with sexual appeal more than those without, but that effect doesn't extend to the brands or products that are featured in the ads . . . [people] liking the ads doesn't influence whether they're going to make a purchase." So yes, skin will still grab people's attention, *but it has little to no effect on their purchase behavior.*[9] In today's era of infinite media, in which the number of brands has multiplied exponentially, people are unlikely to even look at ads, much less remember any particular name. Flashing skin has become a quaint idea whose time is over.

The second truism that's no longer true? "There's no such thing as bad press." In the limited era, consumers were likely to read or hear something (bad or good) and remember key parts but not the full story. As the details faded, often all they recalled was a brand name, which they would likely notice again but not necessarily remember why they knew it. So even bad press had a significant long tail, able to help drive top-of-mind positioning. Today, modern media channels optimize for *context*, so when we do a Yelp, Yahoo, or Google search they'll surface all stories, bad and good. Online ratings and reviews have been added to the mix, making bad press highly contextual to any conversation about your brand. There is no escaping it: bad press is now *very bad.*

Let's look at a third marketing favorite: "right message, right person, right time." This highly trusted idea asserts that to drive consumers to act, you just need to deliver a catchy message with the right timing and targeting. But the multiyear study by WordStream, mentioned at the beginning of this chapter, proves that logic obsolete.[10] Recall that the study looked at more than $1 billion of advertising spent across a two-year period on the Google Ads network by customers using the WordStream platform. With its ability to place tailor-made, dynamic content on the computer screen in front of the consumer at the exact right moment, Google Ads is undeniably the most powerful tool ever to put "right message, right person, right time" to the test. Yet its long-standing ads in the right-hand margins of search results failed consistently to drive consumer action 99.7 percent of the time.

Why? First, consumers don't like messages (remember Doc Searls's statement about ad blocking being the world's "largest boycott"). Second, buyers now have infinite alternatives to help them make their decisions. They trust organic content much more than they do ads, so with limitless content presented at the same time, why would they choose an ad? As Word-Stream CEO Larry Kim told me, customer engagement is no longer the result of ad copy, color, or anything about the message. Engagement is driven purely by how consumers experience your brand in their personal context. What brands recorded the highest engagement rates—four times the average? Those that either had a history with the consumer or offered better experiences for the individual, post-ad. For example, brands with sizzling offers in Google Ads may drive a click, but if the consumer has to fill out a long form to access the gated content, then the experience falters and the consumer leaves.

Finally, consumers' access to infinite trusted content today—media of every kind that is instantly accessible—kills off a fourth long-standing marketing truism: the need for a brand to be "top of mind." My question is, top of *what* mind? Consumers don't remember anything in today's world. Why should they? People offload everything to devices and ask Siri or Alexa to serve up information as needed. In the limited era, when information was much less readily available, being easily memorable was powerfully useful to consumers. But today consumers don't need to remember brands or rack their brains to make decisions. Their devices will search limitless trusted sources and deliver what they want to know, literally into the palm of their hand.

Now that we understand what kind of noise gets noticed today (media within a relevant *context*, not media that relies simply on attracting *attention*), let's break down what that means.

Noise (Media) That's Contextual Is Media That's Permissioned

In a study published by Pew Research in September 2018, 68 percent of US consumers reported that they get at least some of their news from social media (that rises to 78 percent for people under fifty, up only slightly from 2017).[11] That means, in the infinite media era, the dominance of the individual has even begun redefining how a medium itself operates.

Facebook, one of the largest social media platforms in the world, epitomizes that progression. For more than a decade after founding the company, Mark Zuckerberg staunchly defended his famous statement, "We are not a media company." But in 2016, in a public year-end review conducted with Facebook COO Sheryl Sandberg and Mark Zuckerberg, Zuckerberg had to revise that statement. He said in the year-end review Facebook "is not a *traditional* media company,"[12] particularly because it doesn't write the news that appears on it. But he had to admit that the network "does a lot more than just distribute news, and we're an important part of the public discourse." What he's really saying is that Facebook is a media company. It just doesn't look like any other kind of media company, nor operate like any that came before it.

The power behind this reshaping of media stems partly from the "permissioned" nature of individual noise. Back in 1999, email became marketing's newest best medium, and that's when Seth Godin's best-selling book, *Permission Marketing*, appeared. Godin describes how the power of permission drives higher consumer engagement because people more readily engage with things they have asked for over things they have not. In a recent conversation, Godin told me, "It goes back to the lesson we learned as kids. There is a big difference between telling someone a knock-knock joke, and just running up to them and screaming. The essence of human interactivity has always been consensual—it was just erased for 100 years of 'interruption' when media needed to pay for itself. But consumers never liked it." Today permission has become the guiding principle of our entire media environment, not just email. Even noise is permissioned, which means that marketing must constantly be looking for opportunities to achieve permissioned status when creating its experiences.

Permission comes in many forms, such as liking, friending, following, and subscribing. Once individuals give a business permission, marketing can take place in their desired orbits. Consider LinkedIn. The professional network requires that users gain permission to communicate directly with another individual on the platform. But that's only the beginning.

Permissions are layered, which lets LinkedIn drive deeper engagement into a user's personal world.

Say that a former colleague (whom you've permissioned into your network) got a new job. If you've enabled email notifications, LinkedIn will email you about the news, or if you have the LinkedIn app on your phone, it will display a *badge* (better known as the red dot of death, alerting you to one more thing to notice today). It may even go as far as "popping up" a notification on your mobile device's home screen, which would bring the notification directly to your attention. These tactics entice you to visit LinkedIn, so that you can answer the burning question: *what is new with your colleague?* You know it's not earth-shattering news, but curiosity gets the best of you. You want to keep up with your former colleague, so there you find yourself, on LinkedIn and engaged. This is the most impressive part about reaching consumers through permissioned media: you have the power to break through, motivate, and fulfill consumer desires in a way no other marketing concept ever has.

Consider your reaction to a Fitbit notification that gets you to walk one hundred more steps, or the power of a traffic notification from GoogleMaps that alters, en route, your daily drive to work. How about the notification you might receive on your phone while reading this book, letting you know you've got a meeting in ten minutes? The power of individual media to change consumer behavior and motivate a person to act is far greater than any other form of media ever to exist, and none of it is possible without permission.

How *Will Marketers Succeed? Through Experiences— Not Messages*

We've seen how the static messages of the limited media era don't persuade consumers today to act. People find advertising annoying, so they just block it. How, then, can businesses break through to customers? By offering them experiences within their immediate context.

That is the third shift that came with the infinite media era. We've moved into a new world where products and services have become commoditized and experiences are the next evolution in business value. The video ads that automatically play before you can watch a news story on CNN, for example, could be considered an experience, although it's not a desired one. In their book *The Experience Economy*, Joseph Pine and James Gilmore suggest that the highest economic value businesses can create is an experience that helps individuals grow or expand their *possibilities*.[13] These are not traditional notions of customer experience; we're talking about experiences across the business, including pre- and postpurchase.

The example of IKEA in the introduction of this book recounted how the company leveraged its purchase of TaskRabbit to offer customers a more seamless and positive postpurchase experience. The strategy is working. TaskRabbit CEO Stacy Brown-Philpot said in an interview that ". . . more customers now will buy things online through the IKEA web site—and buy more things—because the TaskRabbit service is available."[14] By providing a better experience (in this case, postpurchase), IKEA effectively drove not only more online sales but also more sales in general.

Pine and Gilmore's point is that the highest value a business can produce changes according to the era, in line with the economics of the market. In the early years of commerce, we grew things and sold them. As more things were produced, businesses evolved and learned to process things; and those animals, vegetables, and minerals became commodities. Processing and selling things proved more profitable than just extracting them. Moving forward in time, more products were created, and businesses' value evolved again. Customizing a product turns it into services, and today even those have become commoditized. The authors offer examples such as cellphone plans and dollar menus at fast-food restaurants, which are all sold on price, suggesting those services have become commoditized. Considering this same pattern of market saturation followed by customization, the authors find the customization of a service creates an experience, and they conclude that the customization of an experience to a higher value is an experience able to transform the individual.[15]

Pine and Gilmore's book is twenty years behind us now, and today's era of infinite media has ushered in a new way to create higher economic value (as the authors state in their 2011 updated version): transitioning products and services into experiences able to help individuals transform[16]—like how IKEA partnered with TaskRabbit to provide more than just a bookshelf, offering a seamless personal experience of shopping, delivery, and installation. Essentially, IKEA has transformed the customer from being a worker (delivering and assembling purchases) to being a manager (assigning others to do these tasks).

What does all this mean for marketers? In the infinite, experiential age, where every interaction *is* the experience, *is* the product itself, marketing moves from telling you *about* something to *becoming* part of the thing itself. Think about it: the former is undesirable and nonpermissioned; the latter is hugely desirable and highly permissioned, and consumers will pay for it. To succeed as marketers in this new era, we must focus on desired, permissioned (wherever possible) experiences within the consumer's current context: *contextual* experiences.

Contextual experiences have three fundamental qualities: they are *supported, seamless, and dynamic.* First, to successfully execute contextual experiences, companies must decouple marketing from the product and *support* marketing's function from every level of the company. Marketing therefore becomes a much more encompassing pathway to growth, beyond the limited view of merely increasing sales. The full range of customer experiences becomes the primary focus of not only marketing but also the business itself.

When businesses shift their focus to creating experiences—and buy into a new idea of marketing to do it—their financial outcomes far exceed their peers'. That was a finding from a study by Watermark Consulting in 2016: over a seven-year period, the stock price of auto insurance companies that focused on customer experience outperformed the Dow Jones Property and Casualty Index by 129 points. These companies also outperformed customer experience laggards in their auto insurance vertical by three times. More compellingly, this finding held true for two hundred companies in more than a dozen sectors covered in the study.[17]

Second, contextual consumer experiences are not singular. They are a *seamless* series of highly connected events—audience experience, shopping experience, buying experience, user experience, support experience—the sum of which is much greater than the parts. For individuals, there is just one experience they associate with the business; and because it's permissioned every time, it's one they desire.

Consider IKEA's efforts to craft a seamless experience focus on linking the online (digital) and offline (physical store) experiences across the customer journey—what CEO Jesper Brodin calls going "phygital." To accomplish that, IKEA is opening fewer new stores and encouraging customers to use an app to browse the catalog, virtually experience the product in their homes, navigate through stores, manage their shopping cart, and then hire someone (through TaskRabbit) to deliver and install the item. Such a series of connected experiences helps consumers achieve the goal of each moment, spurring consumer motivation and fostering business growth.

Third, customer experiences must take place in the context of the individual and are therefore *dynamic*. For example, when Room & Board wanted to create a better experience across its owned channels, specifically email marketing and its website, it went directly to its customers to find out how. The company assumed that people came to the site looking for a specific piece of furniture, a table or a sofa, but that wasn't true. People were looking for ways to make their rooms look or function better. They were looking to "complete a room." When Room & Board understood this context, it set about fulfilling the desire of those visitors, *individually.*

Not surprisingly, Room & Board had to develop its website and emails technologically to be dynamically responsive to each person looking to complete a room design. The creation of every experience relied on a series of inputs: artificial intelligence, data from in-store purchases, and online behavior, as well as larger data sets about the behavior of consumers looking at similar products. Ultimately, working with Salesforce Room & Board used algorithms to analyze different customer interactions in real time and create a contextual experience on the fly for each person—consistently—whether that customer was on the website or receiving an email.

As a result, today when customers land on Room & Board's website, they will see a room showcasing the specific look they are seeking. The image is not just a re-creation of their past visits, but a predicted vision of the room they are looking to complete *at the moment.* Within one month of implementing this highly contextual approach, Room & Board increased its online sales by 50 percent, bringing in an additional $700,000 in revenue. But the wins didn't end there. Using the same algorithms that instructed the dynamics of the website, the company upended its email strategy, letting the new contextual algorithm decide what content to deliver and when, to ensure that its emails were created and sent at the exact moment they were desired, driving traffic not only to the website but, quite surprisingly, into stores. That's right. Customers participating in the email strategy made 60 percent more in-store purchases than those not receiving emails. Room & Board also began to notice new consumer behavior from this group: after receiving the email, consumers would walk into the store, phone in hand, to show the image (algorithmically selected for them) to a store employee and ask for directions to directly view the product. *That* is motivation.

It might be easy to dismiss the Room & Board example as a technologically advanced but still highly tactical "right message, right time" execution. But that quick judgment would miss the larger significance. The company's marketing impetus for making these changes to the website and email strategy wasn't to reach a certain sales number; instead, it came out of a commitment to a better customer experience. The fact that this experience increased in-store sales by 60 percent and online sales by 50 percent was outstanding—but a secondary goal—and proof that the context marketing revolution is real.

Although many of us have been slow to acknowledge the change, our old ideas of what marketing was, how we executed it, and what its underlying truths were have all been uprooted, and the ground has been prepared for a new idea of marketing to take hold. All of this means that we need to call into question anything we once did to reach consumers during the limited media era. Those foundations no longer apply. In the infinite media era, both media channels and individuals alike value one thing above all else: the right experience in the right context.

All of which is to say that consumers now have a new decision-making process that transcends defined categories of demographics. This reshapes the way we grow brands and how we think about motivating consumers. Now that I've described the media environment, we will explore its effect on the individual and the new all-powerful consumer in the next chapter, where I will walk you through the decision-making experience of the customer today in real-time, context-based moments.

2.

New Consumer, New Consumer Journey

Marketers have argued for more than a decade about how to bridge the gap between *digital natives* (people born after 1995) and *digital immigrants* (older generations forced to migrate to digital from an analog world). Those terms, coined by Mark Prensky in 2001,[1] have mostly been replaced with *millennials* versus *Gen-Xers* and *boomers*, but the marketing debates continue just the same.

In the infinite media era, however, those distinctions aren't relevant, not when it comes to how we motivate consumers. Similarly, the difference between B2B and B2C marketing has completely dropped away. Why? Because "the medium is the message," as Marshall McLuhan put it.[2] His idea, published decades before the dawn of digital, has been interpreted in a variety of ways. But to use McLuhan's own words, it is the *environment* that changes people, not the technology.[3]

In other words, environments are so powerful, they affect all aspects of life, society as well as individuals. McLuhan went so far as to say that the idea we have of romantic love is nothing more than a by-product of the print media. So it isn't such a reach to think that our idea of marketing is simply a by-product of the limited media era environment. And the rules that applied in that environment—such as distinctions among generations or between types of buyers—no longer hold water today. Our environment changed and so did all of us.

This chapter explores the consumer's new decision-making process and illuminates how we as brands must respond: with modern methods of reaching and motivating consumers.

The New Consumer Transcends Labels

In 2018 new research revealed that virtually all consumers discover products, evaluate them, purchase them, and want them serviced in similar ways, regardless of the individual's age, demographic, or business vertical.[4] This is a new reality that we marketers must adapt to, all while meeting the expectations of a changed consumer whose decision-making process is radically altered *because of the infinite environment* (as McLuhan foretold).

Old Dogs, New Tricks

Many people misinterpreted Mark Prensky's distinction between digital natives and immigrants as "you can't teach an old dog new tricks." But that wasn't his point at all. His goal was to help educational institutions better understand their pupils, whose brains had developed differently because of early exposure to the digital world.

But today we know that the human brain, even older brains, adapts quite quickly to the digital environment. Gary Small, a professor of psychiatry at UCLA and director of its Memory and Aging Center, studied the brain functions of a group of "digital savvy" and "digital naive" subjects as they engaged with modern media, and he discovered just how rapidly this adaptation takes place. Small ran two tests, one to set a baseline for each group and one to test the effect of environment exposure on the digitally naive. He asked the naive group to spend one hour a day online for five days, then return to do the test again. After the second test, Small found that "the exact same neural circuitry in the front part of the brain became active in the internet-naïve subjects.[5] Five hours on the internet, and the naïve subjects had already rewired their brain," in line with the digitally savvy.

So as marketers, we must account for the effects of the media environment on *all individuals*, because individuals all operate similarly within the infinite environment. Segmenting by age or any other demographic will not help you break through to the modern buyer. This is true whether they are millennials or boomers, even the elderly. My grandfather isn't shopping on Amazon, but he's aware of the power of the new environment, so he asks me to check prices for him and make purchases. He has essentially adapted to the infinite media era, and he's never been on the internet—yet.

A more helpful distinction than a person's age comes from researchers David S. White and Alison Le Cornu. Their paper "Visitors and Residents: A New Typology for Online Engagement" offers a more behavior-oriented definition of consumers that isn't tied to generation. Rather than binary opposition, they see consumer behavior as a continuum. At one end are "Visitors," people who hop on and off the internet, using it primarily as a toolbox. At the other end are "Residents," who view the internet as a "place" where they interact with clusters of other people "whom they can approach and with whom they can share information about their life and work."[6]

Today's consumers lie somewhere on this continuum, and people formerly viewed as digital immigrants, or boomers, are engaging with the infinite media environment specifically to change their behavior, because they see the benefits it provides. According to our 2017 Salesforce study (*State of the Connected Customer*) looking at 7,037 global consumers, 72 percent of baby boomers *strongly agree* that new technology keeps them better informed about product choices than ever before.[7] The study also confirms that while there are differences between millennials and other demographic groups regarding expectations, actions, and other factors, the delta between groups is much smaller than traditionally thought. Only a 12 percent gap separated the responses between millennials and baby boomers across the one hundred questions we asked, such as: How willing are you to share personal data for better experiences? How does branded communications in the form of rewards affect your brand loyalty? How important is it to be able to do a price comparison from your mobile device? In short, across the board, our data suggests that if 100 percent of millennials act in a particular way, it's a good bet that 88 percent of baby boomers do too.

Such rapid adoption by all consumers makes sense when you consider the timeline of past media. The written word took millennia to spread; the

The Post-AI Consumer

With infinite media come infinite web pages, emails, answers, and content. Managing that expanse is far past human cognition, however, and so all media channels will soon, if they haven't already, employ AI to help consumers. This even applies to print media since AI allows for personal publications to be printed and sent, based on a number of factors. Lowe's home improvement stores already use AI to create printed mailers that leverage personal in-store purchasing data, website behavior, and weather patterns to produce and send a unique mailer for each person. Today, every interaction a consumer has with the infinite media is first filtered through a layer of AI, which surfaces the most contextual experience to the moment. That new reality is the heuristics of modern consumer behavior. In fact, experts project that by 2025, 95 percent of all interactions between a brand and a consumer will happen via AI.[8] Looking specifically at the five most common media experiences—search, websites, social, email, and voice—we can see how AI is reshaping consumer behaviors, laying the groundwork for how we must respond.

Every search engine, whether it's Yahoo, Bing, or Amazon, is powered by some of the largest and most powerful AI on the planet, which returns to consumers a list of perfect answers in a fraction of a second. This power has already changed consumer behavior in significant ways, again eroding many of our long-standing ideas of consumer behavior and how we respond.

The first major change AI has had on consumers is how they find content: they now understand that search engines are more powerful than brand websites. This is why the average number of consumer page views per session on a website has dropped below two pages. Consumers realize that AI will answer their questions far better than the individuals will themselves by fumbling around on your site. And if they don't instantly arrive at what they're seeking, they simply bounce back to their search.

Responding to this new consumer behavior means rethinking how we design experiences. Experiences like websites are often designed for "flow"—the brand expects a consumer to move from page to page because the individual likes the site's button location or size, its offers, copy, or color. But the data is clear: there is no flow. Post-AI consumers don't go to a second page, because they know that a better experience awaits them elsewhere. This is why marketers in 2019 increased their use of AI on websites by 275 percent,[9] leveraging the AI to create a *personal web experience for each person in real time*. The AI knows what to create by tracking each person's personal behavior, as well as total audience behavior, combining the two data sets to know not just what the person is looking for but also what others looking for that same thing have already engaged with. All of this allows the AI to create the most engaging experience in any moment. There is no need for the consumer to dive deeper into the site to find what he or she is looking for; the AI surfaces it for the consumer.

Email is another great example of how AI is helping to surface the best possible experience. AI already manages your email by filtering out spam and malicious emails, or placing promotional emails in a different folder. Next there is your actual inbox, which does this same thing again. Only emails from businesses and individuals you've previously engaged with make it into your primary inbox folder. If the tool, email program, or messaging application you are using doesn't already do this, it is only a matter of time before it does. The simple reason is AI makes these experiences better for the consumer by helping people filter through the noise, whose levels are ever rising.

Even after AI has filtered an inbox, there's still so much content that people are learning ways to manage the glut on their own. Usually they do this by scanning the subject lines, deleting the nonessentials. That means consumers rely on fewer than one hundred characters of text to determine the email's value. This is a learned behavior of the new world. Marketers must respond by learning new ways of engaging via instant messaging. Rather than crafting mass emails, we should shift to sending communication based on the person's exact place on the journey, a personal experience made just for that moment.

A second significant piece of the post-AI world is social media. In 2015 Facebook stated that each time a person logged on, more than one thousand posts awaited him or her—yet the user may see only a few dozen while scrolling. Again it's AI that determines which ones we see, and some posts have been published minutes, days, months, even years before. So social media feeds are not chronological accounts but rather contextual feeds. Again, consumers are being exposed to the most contextual experience, creating new experiences along their journey. To respond, brands must consider context when crafting social content. A simple meme taking ten seconds to create is just as likely to break through as an infographic you spend three weeks working on. The context is the determining factor of its effectiveness, not the content.

The post-AI consumer isn't just enabled by the technology but changed by it. Now that consumers are being fed only context-based experiences, their desire for those experiences is rising. The new world has changed buyers so fast that they now consider experiences just as important as the product or service you sell. That's why marketing must become the owners and sustainers of all experiences.

printing press took centuries. But by the time we reached the introduction of television, it took only sixty-six years for TV sets to saturate 74 percent of US homes.[10] The next major technological advance, the internet, grew to mass adoption (75%) in thirty years, roughly half the time it took television to reach that point. Finally, social media arrived and was adopted by 74 percent of the population in fourteen years. Messaging applications like Facebook Messenger, WhatsApp, WeChat, and LinkedIn Messenger have already overtaken social media in terms of total use, rising to mass adoption in less than seven years. So what's next? Chatbots have now entered the scene, and 80 percent of US businesses expect to use them by 2020.[11] Augmented reality (AR) was added to iPhone and Android operating systems in 2018,[12] so following the same trajectory, we should expect highly immersive AR experiences to be mainstream with all consumers by the mid-2020s. Not only is new media technology adopted in half the time of whatever its predecessor happened to be, but with the shorter intervals between the introduction of new media, the halving is accelerating too. (For more on what all of this implies, see sidebar, "The Post-AI Consumer.")

B2C and B2B Don't Matter—Risk Does

Assuming a generation gap in consumer behavior isn't the only broad misconception fooling businesses and marketers. Many also believe that B2C buyers are far more affected by the changed media environment than B2B customers. But the same 2017 Salesforce global survey referenced earlier found the opposite: compared with 75 percent of B2C buyers, a full 83 percent of B2B buyers feel more informed than ever before because of technology.[13] In fact, across every category B2B buyers are more affected by the new environment than are their B2C counterparts (see table 2-1).

The same sensitivity holds true around servicing products postpurchase. Our data shows that 60 percent of B2B buyers say it is very important to

TABLE 2-1

B2B vs. B2C attitudes

	B2B	B2C
Technology has made it easier than ever to take my business elsewhere[a]	82%	70%
Technology is redefining my behavior as a consumer[b]	76%	61%
Technology has significantly changed my expectations of how companies should interact with me[c]	77%	58%
I expect the brands I purchase to respond and interact with me in real time[d]	80%	64%

a. Salesforce, *Customer Experience in the Retail Renaissance*, 2018, https://www.salesforce.com/form/conf /consumer-experience-report/?leadcreated=true&redirect=true&chapter=&DriverCampaignId =70130000000sUVq&player=&FormCampaignId=7010M000000j0XaQAI&videoId=&playlistId =&mcloudHandlingInstructions=&landing_page=.
b. Salesforce, *State of the Connected Customer*, 2019, https://www.salesforce.com/company/news-press /stories/2019/06/061219-g/.
c. Salesforce, *State of Marketing*, 2016, https://www.salesforce.com/blog/2016/03/state-of-marketing-2016 .html.
d. Salesforce, *State of Marketing*.

The New Experience Is Multimodal

In 2019, Google proclaimed it had more than one billion virtual-assistant devices in the global market.[14] Each assistant is a new interface to our world, changing the way all consumers communicate and what they desire. Why type a search if you can speak your request? Why click if you can just tell the assistant to buy? The rapid rise of voice recognition, along with drastically improved technical capabilities, is creating newly fluid multimodal conversations. Just as we've become familiar with working through multiple channels—to be where the customers are—now we must go further to ensure those moments are also multimodal: not just communicating in new formats, but also learning to craft entirely new experiences as a result.

Today most of our digital experiences are graphical, meaning that a person engages with images to navigate and accomplish tasks. Think of a website, or your computer desktop. Before the graphical interface, digital experiences were command based. DOS-based commands were required to access programs and run them. Bill Gates changed this with graphical user interface (GUI), and the creation of Windows taught us the power of the click. In the infinite media era, the rise in voice recognition and conversational interfaces means that clicking on websites and navigating through graphical interfaces are going away. Why? Just as GUI was faster than DOS, in many cases a conversation is faster still and better suited to accomplishing the task at hand than, say, pointing and clicking.

For example, it takes me seven clicks to make a payment through my bank's online website. Banks like Ally, with its Assist bot, now allow a consumer to simply tell the bot who to pay and how much. The goal is accomplished with zero clicks, with a fraction of the effort. Conversational interfaces are much faster at accomplishing tasks than GUI in many cases, but not all.

As voice begins to change consumer behavior, we must keep in mind the need for speed. Sometimes it is faster for a consumer to read than to listen. Think of product options as an example. If I asked, "Alexa, what are the latest designs in men's shoes?" I still want to see them because I'm able to make a better determination between products visually than audibly. As marketers, we need to think of how to account for such situational differences. This is where multimodal really comes into play. We must be prepared to create experiences that match consumers' desires, meaning they may ask a question using voice recognition but want the answer displayed on a screen. Conversations today combine all mediums.

Beyond voice, consumers are using new imaging formats to communicate. In her *2019 Internet Trends Report*, Mary Meeker cites Instagram cofounder Kevin Systrom, who believes that "writing was a hack" invented by humans when visual images became more difficult to use for communication.[15] We have always been visual communicators, he wrote; we just stopped for a while until images became easier to create again, as they are today. In the same report, Meeker also shows that in 2017, people created more than one trillion images. And every day we have new formats of imaging "language" to work with, such as emojis, graphic interchange formats (GIFs), and memes.

The point is that consumers are using visuals to communicate more and more, and marketers must adapt, not only by using them ourselves but also by learning how images can open doors for nontraditional communication. For example, if a customer shares an image of your product, the desired reaction from you is likely just a simple "like" (thumbs-up) of the image or emoji. Consumers view such brand actions as a validation that communicates "I hear you" or "Thank you." And again, it isn't just millennials who are engaging in such communication; this is behavior that we have all learned simply by operating in the infinite expanse.

As media channels expand and bifurcate (e.g., Reddit, Quora, TikTok, WeChat, Fortnite), and input methods (voice, images, typing) continue to increase, we marketers will need to keep our focus on what consumers desire to ensure we deliver the experience they want.

receive in-app support, compared with only 43 percent of B2C consumers. Furthermore, 82 percent of B2B buyers say personalized care affects their loyalty, compared with 69 percent of B2C consumers. B2B buyers also hold higher expectations for the digital future. Sixty-three percent of B2B buyers expect their vendors to provide customer service via augmented reality by 2020.

If the differences between B2B and B2C behavior no longer matter in the infinite environment, what does matter? The *perceived risk* associated with a purchase. The riskier the purchase, the greater the consideration consumers will give it and the longer the sales cycle will be. So we should look to classify buyer behavior based on the level of consideration involved in the purchase, rather than the vertical of business or any other factor. Generally, this means traditional B2C purchases are mostly low consideration (less risk), while traditional B2B purchases are high consideration (more risk)—but the exceptions call even this broad stroke into question.

For example, consumers booking an African safari will act much more like traditional B2B buyers because of the risk associated with their decision. There is much less risk in booking a $600 weekend at a hotel three hours from home, compared with $10,000 per week on another continent. Thus, the consumer will give the safari purchase much more consideration and exhibit very different buying behavior. Moreover, even buyers for the same safari product will exhibit different consumer behaviors, based on the risk they perceive. Buyers familiar with the safari market perceive lower risk, and their decision-making process is often shorter.

To work synchronously with the infinite era, business leaders and we marketers must lose our preconceived bias about various categories of consumers and embrace the new consumer decision-making journey, which is based on perceived risk. We must also account for the fact that nearly all decisions are now considered decisions, and that consumers undertake that consideration in a very personal context. (For more perspective on new consumers and their needs, see the sidebar "The New Experience Is Multimodal.")

The New Customer Journey

Every marketer is aware that the modern decision-making process has changed because of longer sales cycles and the demand for more content (to name only two of many factors). We're all trying to make the new demands fit into a nice, clean customer journey. And it isn't just marketers. Consulting firms have put serious research and effort into helping brands understand this shift by publishing their versions of "the new buyer's journey." Frameworks like the Sirius Decision Demand Waterfall break the process into these steps: inquiry (inbound/outbound), marketing qualification, sales qualification, close, and advocacy. Other models use the terms awareness, consideration, purchase, and advocacy.

But given today's environment, those models all make a common error: they see the customer journey as *starting* with brand awareness, embodied in this description from McKinsey & Company: "The consumer considers an initial set of brands, based on brand perceptions and exposure to recent touch points."[16] For consumers today, however, the decision-making process begins long before they have an awareness of any particular brand—and then they progress on a whole different path from the one they moved along during the limited era. In the infinite era, marketers need to understand that the customer's decision-making process (which for our purposes *is* the customer journey) actually begins with a *trigger*: a moment when the individual comes up with an idea to change something.

The Trigger

A trigger could be your boss telling you to find a new tool or a social post from a friend showing you a stunning new pair of eyeglasses. Triggers also might be something emotional, like a fight with your spouse, or physical, like feeling a hunger pang. Regardless of the specifics, the point is that all consumer journeys start with such a trigger.

For marketers, that's a major change in perspective. Instead of trying to force change as we once did, by trying to get people's attention and *make*

Batching: Consumer Behavior in the Infinite Era

Batching is a very human response to infinite media, and it refers to two kinds of behaviors. The first is when a consumer is searching for answers to a question and then gathers that set of answers into one place. The second behavior refers to the way consumers often batch many questions together in short succession. These two behaviors are a big key to motivating the modern consumer. Here is why.

Within each stage of the customer journey the individual has a goal, and that goal changes, depending on the stage. For example, in the *ideation* stage, the goal might be to test an idea and see where the path goes. But in the *awareness* stage, the goal might be to find possible solutions, to be better informed, or to find solution providers—or it could be all three.

The key to motivating customers is to understand how goals are accomplished via batching, and how brands can take advantage of batching behavior in a way that moves a person onto the next question, goal, or stage. For example, if a consumer is in the awareness stage and the goal is to find out "What is the best look in computer bags," the person will look at four different websites for answers and spend a total of just over a minute.[17] So if your brand can be on as many of those sites as possible, it will more likely break through, build the trust, control the narrative, and then be able to guide the consumer to the next stop on the journey.

Batching also refers to the fact that consumers often ask lots of questions in quick succession. Each batch spawns another, then another, going as long as the consumer wishes. So returning to "What is the best look in computer

---

them want something, context marketing harnesses and guides *an existing desire*, one that springs from the trigger.

Think of the trigger as an umbrella-like starting point, from which the consumer then can move to any point along the customer journey, depending on how much information the individual already has about the decision to be made. In other words, triggers jump-start a customer journey or they can restart or continue a journey somewhere along a path already taken.

bags," an article about the latest tech gear may pop up, and the consumer learns that the look this year combines recycled materials with leather. She then scans three more articles and sees that the most popular color is a two-toned black and tan. The consumer now changes her goal to finding the best-quality two-toned bag, which begins another round of batching and finally leads to a purchase. The entire journey might have taken just a few minutes or could have been stopped and restarted over an entire year or more.

By understanding the modern consumer behavior of batching, we marketers can begin to design our content, programs, and experiences to be easily "batchable," which allows us to efficiently and repeatedly meet consumers in the context of their moment and motivate them in a new way.

Batching also suggests we should rethink the role of our public relations departments and any attempts to use mass media to create narrative control over our brands. Also referred to as share of voice, narrative control looks at all forms of media occurring at any one point in time and then measures the prominence of a brand's name. But in the era of infinite media, the only narrative control that motivates the customer journey—and drives demand—emerges from within the batches *the consumer gathers* by taking an extremely intricate and personal path to find answers. Consumers do this not only because they can but also because they trust their own research and experiences *over the messaging of a brand*. That's a critical aspect of today's environment that none of us can afford to miss. We'll explore batching in more detail in part three of this book.

For example, if someone rear-ends your car and takes off your back fender, you'll likely begin looking for an attorney or at the least a body shop. You weren't thinking about auto repair before the wreck. After the wreck it is front and center. That's a trigger that jump-starts a customer journey, taking you all the way to purchasing at least one service. But what if the damage to your car was very minor, a tiny dent and no harm really done? You're not consumed with finding a repair service or lawyer, but you do a few Google searches, ask friends for recommendations, and contact one or two body shops, figuring you'll eventually get the ding fixed—but essentially you've put the process on hold. A few days later, however, one of the body shops sends you an email with an estimate for the repair. That's a trigger that plunges you back to reengaging with the journey but starting at a different point (further into it) from where you began.

So triggers can occur anywhere along the journey and are different for each person. It's also important to note that some triggers are much more powerful than others, and that generally triggers fall into one of two categories: *natural* triggers, which are those that happen to people (like a car wreck) or that they otherwise come upon naturally during the course of their day; and *targeted* triggers, which brands push out directly, such as an email from sales or a chatbot deployed upon a consumer's web visit, or by engaging directly via social media. One of the major roles of modern marketers will be to identify natural triggers along their customers' journeys and work to ensure their brand is part of the journey that the trigger tips off.

Next we'll look at what happens after a consumer experiences a trigger (of either kind), meaning the individual embarks on the six stages of the new customer journey. As I've formulated it, the stages are *ideation, awareness, consideration, purchase, customer,* and then *advocacy.* First, however, note that there's another key aspect of today's consumer behavior that most discussions and models of the customer-journey process miss: I call it batching. Read about it in the sidebar, "Batching: Consumer Behavior in the Infinite Era."

After the Trigger: Six Points along the New Consumer Journey

Once a trigger has kick-started (or restarted) a buyer's decision-making process, the individual journeys through the six stages, as shown in figure 2-1. Note that "t" stands for the triggers that can come into play at any stage; the letters below the "t" represent the six stages of the customer journey, beginning with ideation and ending with advocacy. (Note that although advocacy is also listed as a final stage in the other marketing models I

FIGURE 2-1

The new customer journey

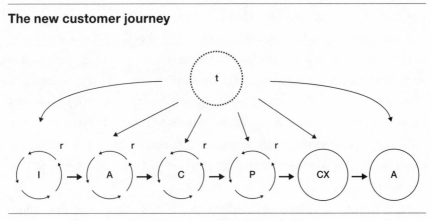

mentioned in this chapter, the way marketers must carry out advocacy in the infinite media era is quite different, as you will see later in this book.) Finally, note that in the figure the letter "r" signifies the risk involved in the decision, and the arrows surrounding each stage denote batches. (Recall how the number of batches increases according to how risky the consumer perceives the purchase decision.)

Now let's look briefly at just the first four stages of the journey: ideation, awareness, consideration, and purchase. Later, in part three, we'll explore each of these stages in detail, along with the fifth and sixth stages (customer and advocacy).

The Ideation Stage

Think about it: because consumers have access to so much information, their search for a solution does not start by assembling a group of vendors, as McKinsey and others imply. Rather, today's *context*-based journey starts with a trigger and then moves to *ideation*: the consumer has a goal in mind and begins to solve it. The trigger might be a new driving regulation or a demand from your spouse to tidy up. That kicks off clusters of questions and answers that help consumers first clarify their thinking—"How to buy curtains" or "Ways to comply." This goal is accomplished via the batches that I describe in the sidebar "Batching: Consumer Behavior in the Infinite Era." All of which brings up an important point: even though businesses usually treat all website visitors as people already interested in their product, the opposite is true. A full 96 percent of the people who visit a website are not ready to buy the product; they're simply conducting research.[18]

Where old marketing models stood on the belief that advertising could both spark the idea and drive product demand, today's marketing task is very different: we must do everything possible to uncover the voluminous *questions* that consumers pose every day, and be in those moments helping them to achieve their goal. Brands that can't do that won't survive. The many, many questions become the batches that naturally construct the modern buyer's journey (with the number of batches determined by the level of risk).

In addition to queries made through various search engines, many people use apps such as Pinterest, Evernote, and Houzz, which are all what I think of as "ideation apps" that help them form and manage their visions and plans. People using those apps along their journey may be in the early stages, but those people have a higher propensity to buy. A recent study showed that 93 percent of Pinners (people who use Pinterest) use the app because they either plan to purchase or are in the process of making a purchase.[19]

As your customers distill their ideas, they discover on their own what they need, and they assemble their own buying criteria. That's when they encounter vendors, as well as the customers of those vendors, through their brand content, and copious reviews. In ideation, customers fully experience several different brands, and the brands that are best able to help their consumers achieve their goal are given the ability to guide them toward the next stop on the journey, and motivation begins.

That's why recognizing and accounting for the ideation phase is so critical to context marketing. Even McKinsey recognizes its importance, although unaccountably it doesn't articulate this stage in its own model. But McKinsey research concludes that brands encountered in the initial stages of a buyer's journey have up to a three times greater chance of generating a purchase than brands that aren't part of those stages.[20] The earlier you are able to establish trust, the greater the effect downstream.

What does all of this mean? That brands should be spending a significant amount of their time and energy preparing and positioning themselves to support ideation by the consumer.

They need to be everywhere buyers are looking, and they need to provide the kinds of answers that meet or exceed consumer expectations, with the tactical focus of guiding them forward.

For example, let's say that a thirtysomething man, Bill, decides to update his wardrobe. That's his trigger. Most likely, Bill will hop online to seek out the best ways to refresh his look, and what he finds will *set the criteria for his journey*. Bill searches for "best fall fashions" and first finds an article on Elle.com talking about the hot new fashions for women. Bill hops back to Google and appends his search with "for men" and tries again. Then he scans the results page and clicks on a few articles he'd like to read. He looks at the first two and notices most of the suggestions require him to buy a full wardrobe. Then he reads the third, an article suggesting that new shoes are an easy way to get the "fall look," and his number-one criterion now becomes a new pair of shoes. His idea solidified, Bill now enters the awareness stage as he begins his journey to find a pair of shoes.

Note, however, that just as easily as Bill was drawn to buying new shoes, his journey could have led him to achieve a new look in a different way—by buying a linen shirt, getting an expensive haircut, or buying houndstooth pants. We will return to this topic of ideation in part three, but for now understand that it is absolutely critical to be as early as you can in your customers' journey. The earlier you can help them achieve a goal, the earlier you can build trust and drive greater demand for your brand.

The Awareness Stage

Once Bill is clear on the idea of shoes as the way to refresh his wardrobe, he has a new goal: to find out what shoes will work best. To accomplish this goal, he has to become aware of the options, thereby entering the *awareness* stage to further refine his search to shoe styles and materials.

Again, and likely even in the same browser session, Bill does another search, "best shoes for fall, men." But once again he's faced with lots of content options, and he decides to scroll through the image results, hopping back and forth between sites, each time noticing a shoe, clicking the image, and visiting the site. Finally he realizes the shoe style he wants is called "monk strap." He goes back to Google and searches "best monk strap shoe, men," and he goes directly to the image search. At last he sees the perfect pair, but his journey is far from over.

The Consideration Stage

Bill is now sure he wants this monk strap look, and he has a specific shoe in mind. But because Bill has narrow feet, he has a few more questions before he can buy the shoes online. For example, do they run wide or narrow and how well made are they. Bill quickly batches these actions together as he checks the shoes' quality by reading three reviews. He is comfortable with this brand from the reviews so he proceeds to check the fit, using the True Fit application he finds on the brand's own site.

Additionally, Bill might search for different colors and options in this stage. If these questions are easily asked on the site, he will stay there—if not, he will return to Google to gather another batch of answers. Finally, Bill has narrowed down his desire and is ready to take the next step: fulfilling that desire.

The Purchase Stage

During the purchase stage, consumers focus on final details of the transaction: price, delivery method, and so forth. To be sure he's getting the best price, Bill does a search using the specific details of the shoes he seeks: "blue suede monk strap shoes 10M Johnston Murphy under $200." Again Bill is given a list of highly contextual results in a fraction of a second. He sees that all the prices are the same. But Bill is a serious discount shopper and does one more thing. He searches for a "coupon" for the shoe company and finds a 10 percent off deal posted on a couponing site. Finally, Bill navigates to his shopping cart and buys the $200 shoes. When they arrive, he's thrilled to feel that he truly has completed a new look for himself.

Bill's entire journey consisted of multiple batches of answers and lasted a short period of time—likely minutes, not hours. His level of consideration (midlevel, not high or low) for a consumer product is the result of his ability to ask the questions, and his motivation to purchase the shoes was a direct result of the experience he found on his journey. Now Bill's customer journey moves into the brand's court; it's up to that shoe brand to create an amazing *customer* experience, with the hope of creating an *advocate* out of Bill. But we'll get to that in part three. The point here is to show how many different brand experiences Bill encountered in quick succession. Batching within each stage of the consumer journey is a heuristic behavior (taught to us by our media environment—that's right, McLuhan again) that increasingly *all buyers* exhibit. Why? Because this is how consumers choose to use the considerable power they wield in the infinite era.

The idea of the customer journey is not new; what's new is the way we must approach it, manage it, and use it. Brands must embrace consumers' freedom and realize that they feel most motivated when they're guided along their *own* journey. The full expression of that journey happens over time. It's the by-product of brand experiences that somehow break through and deeply touch the individual, because that person has been met in his or her personal context of the moment and has been moved to take the next step in the context-based revolution.

Next, part two will examine the five elements of context, so we'll know what each moment must entail.

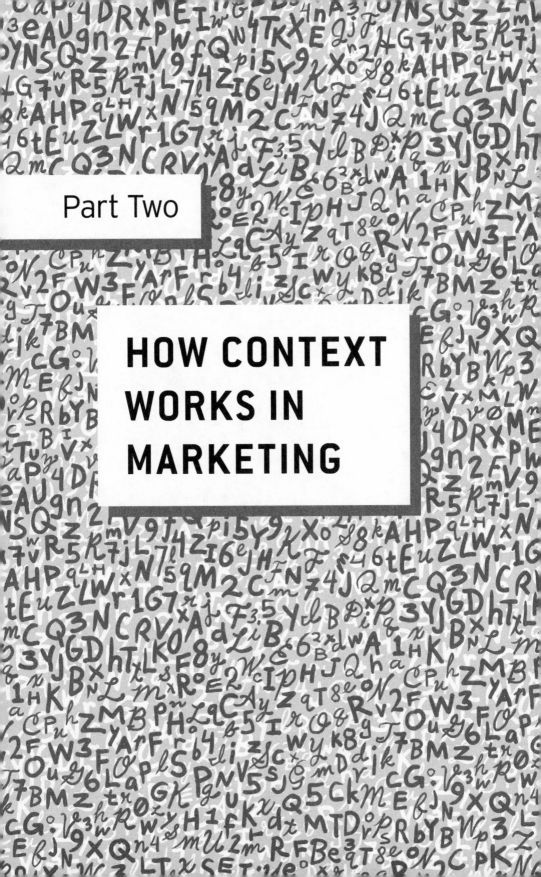

Part Two

HOW CONTEXT
WORKS IN
MARKETING

3.

The Context Framework

Breaking Through the Noise

Back in the limited media era, marketing meant airing a car commercial during an evening TV sitcom. Everyone watching the sitcom would see the ad, but only a fraction of those viewers may be interested in buying a new car. Such advertising still appears today, of course, but as we learned in part one, it isn't very effective in the infinite media era. Why? Because a car ad flashed on a screen while someone's trying to unwind in front of a favorite TV show isn't contextual. That is, it isn't relevant to what the consumer is doing at that moment in time, and most likely it isn't welcome either. So people exercise the infinite choices they have and simply record their favorite show to watch later (if it's not already on Netflix or Hulu or the like)—and then fast-forward through the commercials.

As we saw in part one, context marketing breaks through where traditional marketing can't: it meets consumers where they are (rather than trying to attract their attention) by fulfilling their expectations in a particular moment. But it also creates a series of connected moments that incrementally guide customers toward the next step in their particular customer journey. Remember the ways we saw how Tesla does exactly that—versus what the car ad airing during a sitcom accomplishes.

To review, context marketing motivates customers by recasting our definition of *who* the players are (the role of marketing), *how* we market (the execution of marketing), and *what* we do (the *scope* of marketing). Over the next five chapters of part two, we'll examine that *what*: the context. This notion of context is the heart of the context marketing revolution.

To help you and your brand adopt this new idea of marketing—and become a high-performing organization—I created a framework for achieving and measuring the potential context of a moment. Specifically, to meet customers in their context, marketers need to foster customer experiences that are (1) available, (2) permissioned, (3) personal, (4) authentic, and (5) purposeful.

We will look at that framework momentarily, but first let's understand that breaking through the noise and meeting consumers where they are is only the beginning. Rather, it's the *cycle* of context that allows us to build reliable and sustainable pathways that connect our brand with our audience members throughout their journey.

The Context Cycle

One of the biggest differences between our current and past eras is the idea of memory. Not our personal memory, but rather the environment's memory. Limited media had no memory. It didn't know if you read last month's issue of a newsletter. Infinite media does. That's the memory that gets tapped to determine context. Each experience and associated experiences are tracked by AI, which is simultaneously listening to consumers' engagement to determine future outcomes. In this way, context is a cycle. Where context breeds engagement, the engagement signaling greater context increases its future reach.

In this compounding effect, a brand, its audience, and the experiences they create together continually achieve greater context and more reliable reach. Over time, those three parts working together do more than just elevate a single moment. They raise the likelihood that future experiences— like the next Google search, email, or social post—will break through as well. To understand how the cycle works, we need to start with understanding how the AI that's present in all our devices and programs operates.

The AI is always looking for ways to serve up contextual experiences to the user. To determine context, it looks at a wide range of factors, such as who created the experience and what the topic is. Also, who is the user who's engaging with it? A mom? A business owner? Has the individual engaged with similar experiences? Have people similar to the individual engaged with those experiences? The more of such factors AI can identify between the individual and the experience, the greater the context, and the more likely it is to break through. Note that this data is tracked and recorded and referenced continuously, with each engagement added to the ledger, which alters future outcomes.

This cycle is not new; it has always been in play for web pages and search engine optimization. Breaking through in a Google search results page is a combination of topical relevance and how engaging the experience was. Did people click through, visit the site, and then instantly leave? Or did they spend ten minutes on the site looking at multiple pages? And breaking through means engagement with not just the site's content but also the backlinks, shares, likes, comments, time on page, and more. These signals are the compounding factors that ensure our brand experiences are more readily found along a person's journey. Again, they also ensure that all similar experiences are more likely to be seen, not just that one. In other words, past engagement suggests to the AI that there will be future engagement— and the cycle continues.

All modern media now follows this same model. Social posts are exposed to more people as more people engage with them. Email filters begin to notice if you open and engage with emails from a particular person or vendor, moving them and placing them in the "important" tab. It's a cycle of context that's driven by engagement.

Consumer engagement is a very strong compounding factor, but that is not where the cycle starts—only what keeps it going. The cycle starts by creating experiences that consumers want to engage with. It starts with the five elements of context, and those elements are compounding too. I will dive into each element later in this section, but first let me show you a simple example of how they work together.

Two of the five elements are *available* and *permissioned*. Both are great things on their own, but when combined they have greater power. An available experience exists and can be served up, but if you have permission from the individual to access personal data, you can leverage that information to enhance the experience, compounding the context of the moment by making it more personal. In this same way, each of the five elements compounds to create greater context.

The reliability of context marketing comes from that compounding nature. The more context you create, the more engagement you drive. The more engagement you drive, the more likely that the experience, and others, will break through. With a strong foundation of why we need to focus on context, and how context cycles work to reliably deliver our experiences, let's look at the individual elements of the context framework.

The Context Framework

The framework of the five elements of context—brand experiences that are available, permissioned, personal, authentic, and purposeful—allows you to meet your audience in ever-greater context (see figure 3-1). That is, the more of these elements your brand experience incorporates and combines, the more contextual it will be.

Before I walk you through the framework elements, let's take a quick look at how the framework functions. It is best to view each of the elements as a mini continuum, from least to most contextual. The point where the axis connects to the center of the framework is least contextual. For example, on the permissioned element, the center represents no permission, while the outer edge would be explicit permission. Think of the continuum as a guide to help you see ways you can increase the context of any moment by either moving further out on any one element or adding others.

You can also use the framework to evaluate an experience. By working through each of the elements and marking where on each continuum your experience falls, you will be able to better see why the experience was lackluster and how to improve it. When plotting an experience, the more contextual an experience, the larger the web will be.

As you can see in figure 3-2, the most contextual experiences make a complete web, as in the diagram on the far right.

FIGURE 3-1

The context framework

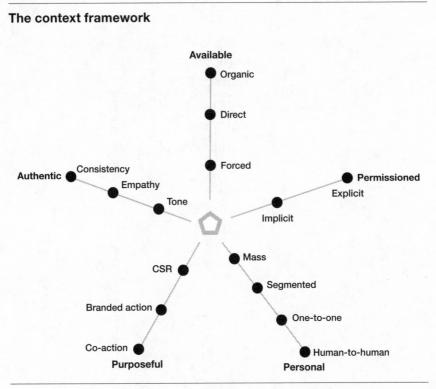

Now let's take a brief look at each of the elements, which we'll explore in depth in the five chapters that follow.

Element 1: Available

An experience cannot break through to anyone unless it's available. Traditional marketing uses a forced approach to make brand experiences available to the largest number of people possible, and the more captive the audience, the better. Context marketing couldn't be more the opposite: its ultimate goal is to help people accomplish their task at hand or achieve the value they seek *in the moment*. Rather than reach masses, context marketing aims to make a single, human-to-human connection at the most opportune moment.

In my framework, available focuses on the delivery method you choose for your brand experience. Do you force it on to people, or do they find it

FIGURE 3-2

Plotting an experience with the context framework

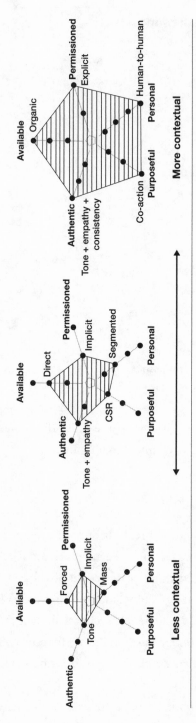

on their own? How the experience is delivered often determines how trusted it is and how likely it is to drive action. At the lowest end of the available continuum are forced experiences—magazine ads, billboards, pop-up ads. Next are direct experiences, which can range from email to social media engagements. The apex of organic experiences are found by the individual in his or her own time.

Element 2: Permissioned

As we discussed in part one, people more readily engage with things they have asked for (permissioned) over things they have not. Much of the interaction that will help your brand and content appear in social feeds and open up direct communication channels. Permission comes in two main forms: implicit and explicit. Implicit permission results when an individual contacts your brand first, such as when the customer has abandoned items on your site's shopping cart and you follow up with a retargeting ad. Permission is implicit here because, wittingly or not, the consumer has given you the information you need to engage with him or her.

Explicit permission involves a defined action taken by a consumer that says, "Yes, I want to be in contact with your brand," such as following, friending, or subscribing. Explicit permission gives your brand access to personal data and a range of new, direct delivery options.

Once your brand has opened a permissioned path, whether implicit or explicit, the context your brand can achieve increases substantially. Chapter 5 focuses on how to gain permission on various channels and how that permission lays the groundwork for becoming more personal, the next element in our framework.

Element 3: Personal

The personal element encompasses every effort you make to tailor your brand experience to an individual person. Obviously, access to personal data allows your brand experience to be the most personalized, but the personal element goes beyond how personalized you can make an experience to *how personally you can deliver it.*

Here we begin to see how direct delivery (see the available element), enabled by the permissioned element, opens the door for brands to go past simple one-to-one marketing and reach the apex of context: human-to-human. This new frontier of marketing enlists your employees, fans, and brand advocates to become a platoon of brand extenders, who build brand relationships in new and distributed ways. In part three we will look at the technology used to scale personal efforts and compound the effects of the first three elements of available, permissioned, and personal.

Element 4: Authentic

Authentic, a popular word these days in plenty of disciplines, generally means that something is genuine or original. The underlying judgment of whether something is an authentic experience often boils down to satisfying an expectation: Is the experience using the right voice? Is it empathic with its audience? Are consumers seeing a brand experience congruent with the media channel they are using (what they expect to see)? To meet the demands of the authentic element, your brand experience must deliver on all three measures.

This is harder than it sounds. The infinite era has new and constantly changing media and mediums, and we cannot look to the past as a guide for using them. Creating authentic brand experiences thus challenges us to leverage voice, empathy, and channel consistency to meet the consumer expectations associated with our ever-changing media landscape. All of this makes authentic the most subjective element of the five: what is authentic in your eyes might not be viewed that way by all of your audiences. Also, just because an experience appears authentic does not guarantee it will break through, which makes it difficult in retrospect to determine whether the experience was considered authentic. Nevertheless, authenticity is often what separates success from failure in your brand experience, even when the three previous elements have been achieved at their most contextual. Authentic also demands a shift away from rigid brand guidelines and approved language toward an adaptable, often on the fly, conversational approach that will provide audiences with brand experiences they will delight in discovering.

Element 5: Purposeful

The first four elements of context help us understand what it takes to deliver an experience (make it available) the individual wants to have (it must be permissioned), delivered by another human (be sure it's personal), in a way that meets expectations (it must be authentic). However, the individual buyer still has to engage, repeatedly, to keep the pathway open and to progress to the final stages of the customer journey as described in chapter 2, such as becoming an advocate for your brand. Quite a TALL order. That's where the fifth element of context, purposeful, comes in to grease the joints by *naturally* motivating significant, even physical, audience engagement.

Purposeful brand experiences range from corporate social responsibility (which basically makes people feel better about you as a brand) to a brand-defining purpose that thematically guides all campaigns to coaction: when your brand and individuals in your audience participate in a brand experience together. Purposeful experiences allow the brand to converse on topics beyond the product or service it offers, which creates deeper, more contextual customer relationships.

For example, the company GoPro makes cameras, yet rarely ever talks about cameras in its marketing. Instead, it focuses on the thrill of adventure, a purpose it shares with its audience by posting an audience member's (read: customer's) "Photo of the Day" every day. By employing the purposeful element, GoPro has amassed fourteen million followers on Instagram, which is almost ten times the combined audiences of the much more established camera brands Canon and Nikon. Because the photos by GoPro's audience are so engaging, the social channels are more likely to show the company's other content too, because engagement breeds engagement. The upcoming chapter on the purposeful element showcases what GoPro and other brands do to perpetuate a long customer life cycle, including opportunities to share activity (coactions)—all in the name of a greater purpose.

Each of the next five chapters will explore the elements of context in greater depth, including examples of brands that are hitting the ball out of the park when it comes to the "what" of context marketing. These examples will show you how to develop a new idea of marketing and create highly contextual brand experiences—ones that engage your audience where they are, in the moment, and in ways they expect and desire. So let's get to it—starting with available.

4.

Available

Helping People Achieve the Value They Seek in the Moment

For a brand experience to break through the noise, a customer needs to see it or hear it or feel it—and ideally all three. In other words, it needs to be available, which is the first of the five elements composing the context framework. Making your brand experience available means consciously choosing and orchestrating how you deliver it, *so that your customers gain the value they seek in the moment.* That is the ultimate definition of meeting customers in their context.

And make no mistake: how people encounter a brand in the infinite media era greatly affects their attitude toward it. Do you force it on people, or do they find it on their own? How you deliver the experience will determine how much the consumer trusts the brand and how likely he or she will act on that trust and engage with you. Get the context right, and your audience is much more likely to take an interest in your brand.

Traditional marketing uses a forced approach to make brand experiences available to the largest number of people possible, and the more captive the audience, the better. Think about the last time you sat in a movie theater while a commercial played on the big screen before the feature began. Maybe you found it entertaining, or maybe it was overly loud and annoying. But it's unlikely you remember today much about it, and even more unlikely that it motivated you to engage with that brand. Context marketing couldn't be more the opposite: its ultimate goal is to help people accomplish their task at hand. Rather than reach masses, context marketing aims to make a single, human-to-human connection at the most opportune moment.

This brings us to an important point: when it comes to the ways marketers make their brands available, there's a *range of efficacy* in their methods, a continuum between least effective (traditional marketing) and most effective (context marketing). That is, even if you as a marketer are unable to make an immediate leap to the most effective path to availability, there are ways to work with where you are, specifically in the middle of the continuum.

I identify three points along that continuum, three methods of making your brand experience available (see figure 4-1). At the lowest end are *forced* experiences: magazine ads, billboards, pop-up ads, or the commercial you sat through in the movie theater. Next on the continuum are *direct*

FIGURE 4-1

The context framework (available)

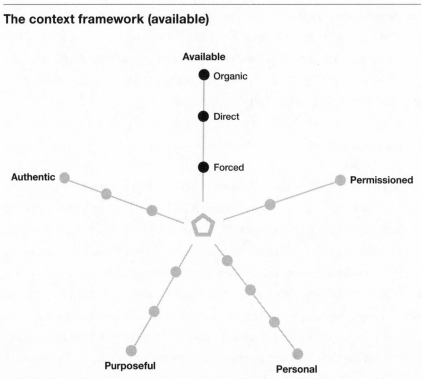

experiences, which can range from email to social media engagements. Finally, there's the apex of effectiveness in the infinite era—*organic* experiences, which are found by individuals in their own time.

Understanding the distinctions among these methods of availability, their power to break through in particular moments, and how to use them to create better experiences across the customer life cycle is the first step to becoming a contextual marketer.

The Forced Experience: Demanding Attention

Forced experiences are the least contextual, because they are one-way. They are designed to work *on* consumers, trying to distract their attention and compel them to buy. When people are forced to sit through your brand experience—your commercial, your click-through ad—you've demanded their attention but you likely didn't really get it. Rather, you purposely delayed what your audience members really wanted to see: the movie, not your ads.

The problem with a forced experience is that it gives little thought to context, which is all that the viewer really cares about. Yes, you might have considered the context of your content: whether the main event that follows your brand experience, such as highlights from a recent sporting event, will likely attract an audience similar to yours. But you still haven't given thought to the context of what an individual viewer is looking for *in that moment*. Nearly all of the creative effort is placed on the message you will broadcast, not the experience you are creating for the viewer. That perspective, in a nutshell, is the difference between traditional and contextual marketing.

For years, forced availability was powerful, and it catapulted many brands into superstardom: Pillsbury, Energizer batteries, Kellogg's cereals, and many others.[1] Even ten years ago, people still expected to sit through forced ads, but now that we are well into the infinite media era, consumers have gotten used to having control. They don't easily tolerate being forced to watch or click anything. In fact, research recounted in an *Atlantic* article found that people are more likely to survive an airplane crash than to click on a banner ad![2] Most often, forced ads get skipped (when possible), ignored, or blocked by software. That isn't to say that a fifteen-minute short video, for example, can't be part of a contextual customer journey. But it would have to be thoughtfully connected to the individual's experience in that moment, and it shouldn't be forced on him or her.

The Direct Experience: Delivering a Message

Direct brand experiences, such as email, messaging applications, and social media engagement, offer more context than forced messages because they are conversational channels that allow brands to work directly *with* people rather than making them watch or listen. These are experiences that happen directly between a brand and an individual, delivered to one of several types of inboxes, including the feeds and messaging applications used on social media platforms.

The increasing use of privacy controls by consumers means that direct experiences almost always require marketers to gain permission to deliver directly to someone's inbox of choice. The permissions hurdle makes direct experiences more contextual, but it also requires an extra layer of creativity. Chapter 5 explains ways to gain permission, but right now we're going to get clear on the most contextual kinds of direct experiences, so you'll know what to do with permission once you get it.

Direct marketing used to be simply forced messages to individuals that were delivered at set intervals by either email or the postal service. Rather than seeking permission, marketing departments usually just purchased from third parties addresses that were *approximately* their audience. These mediocre lists were the backbone of direct marketing efforts for years.

The infinite media era has changed all of that. Direct marketing today runs continually—not at set intervals—and it is permissioned and creates value for recipients in the moment they encounter it. There's no single goal or call to action. Rather, direct brand experiences are created at various points along the buying path and work together to move people along the customer journey. By providing the next piece of information or knowledge the consumer needs, when needed, brands guide, inspire, and motivate individuals. Ultimately, the most contextual direct experiences become human to human, which we'll learn about in the chapter 6 discussion of the framework element "Personal."

Although not as ideally fashioned for the infinite era as are organic experiences (as we'll learn in this chapter), direct marketing experiences can be tweaked and broadened to move them up the continuum to greater levels of contextual consumer engagement.

Expand Your Idea of Direct to Make Your Brand More Available

Direct marketing has moved past simple emails and posts to include all of today's methods of engagement provided by social media, such as likes, comments, shares, mentions, and direct messages. Each of those methods gives marketers a new way to make themselves available to their audiences, both proactively *and reactively*. Let's look at some specific strategies that marketers have used successfully.

Engage with User-Generated Content

Traditional direct marketing is proactive: the brand typically reaches out first. This idea is still valid, but it's important to add reactive brand experiences too. Direct marketing is very powerful in these moments because the consumer has already created the context for marketing to engage by posting a brand image, for example, on social media. Marketers can then reactively create a brand experience by commenting on the post or sharing a published post on the brand's own channel. Many marketers still find it hard to believe that consumers want brands to engage with their social media posts, but most people will acknowledge a brand's reaction, even if the brand wasn't tagged purposely. Take the example from Good Humor in figure 4-2:

Jen Dalton did not mention Oreo's cobrand Good Humor in her tweet, but Good Humor likely had an automation "listening" for keywords associated with the launch of its new venture with Oreo. When the automation "heard" what it was listening for and brought it to the attention of Good Humor's marketing department, it engaged in two ways: it first

FIGURE 4-2

Source: Good Humor Instagram feed.

liked the post and second wrote a comment to the author of the post, Jen. While some brands might refrain from engaging unless expressly mentioned, Good Humor bet on its friendly voice being well received, and it was. Jen liked Good Humor's comment. (I'll go deeper into listening and other automations in chapter 9.)

If this seems like a negligible interaction, it's not. These engagements are personal acknowledgments that users of social media are seeking. You are fulfilling a customer's (or future customer's) immediate desire *in the context of the moment.* In social media language, a "like" is an affirmation saying "I hear you," "I'm with you." When a user likes a comment, it is shorthand for "Thank you" or "I agree." Brief exchanges on social media channels can also include the use of emojis that convey messages instantly, such as "I love it," "That makes me mad," or "That's hilarious"—all of which are phatic ways of acknowledging the author of the post and perhaps prompting an exchange with each other. Such small, direct engagements allow brands to stay front and center in the lives of their audience in new ways and *in context.*

Parlay the Power of "the Mention"

Mentions are another great direct method for making your brand available contextually on social media. The mention allows anyone to directly associate a person with a brand experience either immediately at the time it is posted or later on. The LinkedIn post from Vince in figure 4-3 illustrates how this works:

In creating this brand experience for his employer, SBI, Vince mentions Jill and Sarah directly, which is why their names are in bold. When Vince hits the "Post" button, Jill and Sarah are notified directly of their mention, while Jill's and Sarah's followers might see it in their main LinkedIn feed, driving them to view Vince's post. The more interaction Vince's post gets, the better the chances of it appearing in the feeds of Jill's and Sarah's connections. This means it was very helpful to Vince for Jill to mention Jamie in the comments section, after the story was published. Jamie's response to Jill's mention of him provides the needed interactivity to boost the post's stature and make it more widely available.

Again, this interaction might appear inconsequential to those not familiar with how social media works. And again, it's not. Here's how to view it: Jill and Sarah participated in the event, so Vince hardly needs to make them aware of it. He is mentioning them to reach the hundreds, if not thousands, of connections in Jill's and Sarah's networks. It's no accident that the content was shared by Vince and not by his company (SBI). The human-to-human conversation makes this brand experience available to a larger audience in a much more personal way (coming in chapter 6) than a post from the company announcing that they "had a great time at their event!" Vince's post also exemplifies a new type of direct marketing where employees,

FIGURE 4-3

advocates, or other brand extenders are able to make content available directly and permissioned in ways that are more difficult for a brand to create on its own.

While Vince had his reasons, Jill had a slightly different reason for using the mention. She may be doing some contextual marketing for herself as a presenter, and Jamie may be someone she knows is interested in the topic. Or perhaps Jamie works for a company where Jill would like to make inroads. We'll never know, but Vince undoubtedly benefited from Jill's action, and Jill likely did too.

Drive Interaction within Private Messaging

Likes, shares, comments, and mentions all happen in the public space. All of these social media platforms also have a private form of communication through direct messages. Messaging applications became the most used aspect of social media back in 2015, and now every channel has some form of it: Facebook Messenger, LinkedIn Messaging, WeChat, Twitter Direct Message, and Instagram Direct, to name a few. The good news for contextual marketing is that people aren't only messaging friends and family; they're also engaging with brands more and more through messaging, as the evidence shows.

Facebook IQ conducted a study on the use of mobile messaging with 12,500 people across the world. It found several promising trends among the people surveyed:

- Sixty-three percent said that their messaging with businesses has increased over the past two years.

- Fifty-six percent would rather message than call a business for customer service.

- Sixty-one percent like personalized messages from businesses.

- More than 50 percent are more likely to shop with a business they can message directly.[3]

Where email has a lot of competition, messaging applications are fairly void of brand interactions, even though people are open to engaging with brands there. This makes them a greenfield with a lot of room to experiment with creating contextual brand experiences there. Here are a few examples to show why they are so powerful.

Jay Baer, who runs the marketing agency Convince and Convert, told me his company recently tested using Facebook Messenger. The company found that messages sent via the social messaging channel were opened ten times more than the emails it sent, and those individuals who opened the social messages were five times more likely to click, share, or engage with the content than their email counterparts receiving the same content. Similarly, HubSpot, a marketing technology provider, offered people interested in its content the option to access it in two ways: either fill out the form or skip the form and get the content via Facebook Messenger. People who chose the Messenger option were 242 percent more likely than those who chose email to open the message (33% open rate for email compared with an 80% open rate for Messenger) and 609 percent more likely to engage (2.1% click rate in email compared with a 13% click rate in Messenger) with the content.[4]

And here's a bonus takeaway: people really hate to fill out forms. Give them another option, and they'll take it.

Absolut Vodka was way ahead of the curve on this one. It combined the power of targeted digital advertising with its ability to engage individuals through Facebook Messenger. First, Absolut posted a highly targeted ad on Facebook offering a free drink to people who engaged. The ad was connected to Messenger, guiding users into an experience where they could converse with a chatbot and claim their free drink. The net result was a 4.7 times lift in sales for the brand compared with Absolut's other efforts (see figure 4-4).

The power of making direct experiences available in a multitude of ways that land correctly with your audience is what drives contextual "direct marketing." That said, traditional forms such as email and direct mail should not be ignored. They are still very powerful, but as consumers begin to move from just one inbox (email) to many (social + email), brands will soon be migrating more and more to targeted engagements in direct messaging channels.

Use Automations to Make Direct Methods Available Anytime

While direct methods are not the pinnacle of the context framework (we'll get to that with "Organic"), they do have a serious advantage in that they can be automated. Recall the Good Humor example in this chapter—the company had an automation "listening" for keywords, which is just one kind of marketing automation. There are many automated moments that can be tailored to execute brand experiences at a specific moment, to a specific person, triggered by almost anything.

In the simplest terms, automation allows marketers to shift from starting every conversation with an identified segment in the same way to having

FIGURE 4-4

Source: https://blog.hootsuite.com/facebook-messenger-ads/.

bespoke conversations with each individual from the get-go, at scale. Brands that are using this kind of automation with email communication were found by ANNUITAS to produce 451 percent more qualified opportunities over traditional direct email tactics.[5] That is, the highly personal, one-to-one emails used to automatically nurture each person from his or her initial interest up to the point of being ready to purchase is four times more effective at generating business than any other email method.

This corroborates our Salesforce 2018 *State of Marketing* research, which found high-performing marketing organizations to be 9.7 times more likely to use automations than underperformers are.[6]

All direct methods, including email, direct mail, and direct social interactions, gain in their ability to reach greater context when they are executed automatically. Automations allow sets of conditions to be defined, such as in the case of Good Humor: when someone mentions the words

Oreo and *flavor*, the automation takes a predefined action. It alerts the marketing team to the post, so someone can engage with it. These "listening" automations create a rich range of conversations that brands can now join—and they can even distribute the notifications to the proper teams (sales topics can be sent directly to sales, support questions to the support queue, and so on).

While automations are powerful, they do require a new investment in technology and a new set of tactics, which I'll cover in detail in part three.

The Organic Experience: Interaction and Lots of It

Consumers are much easier to engage when it is their idea to interact with a brand in the first place. That is why organic experiences represent the pinnacle of the available element in our context framework. Brands create an experience that connects with people exactly when they want that experience. That moment might occur almost anywhere, when someone is searching on Google, shopping on Amazon, or perusing Facebook. Or perhaps they're browsing in a store or sitting at home on a laptop or using a tablet at an airport. At the very moment an individual searches for information related to our brand, it is our job as context marketers to be found and to interact. That's what it means to craft an organic experience.

Some brands have built their entire business by focusing on organic brand experiences. The startup wristwatch brand Daniel Wellington focused exclusively on Instagram, relying on the organic nature of the platform to reach its audience contextually and motivate those people to learn more. The strategy worked. In its first four years of operation, the company sold more than one million watches.[7] Focusing on organic search engine rankings—also known as inbound marketing—is also a powerful way to build brands and drive business. Arbor, a senior living community operator with more than thirty communities, reports that 64 percent of all new residents arrive after finding Arbor organically through searches.[8]

I'm using the word *organic*, but perhaps it should be in quotation marks. Because when your brand experience is made available organically, it nevertheless has been served to individuals in your audience algorithmically.

Chasing algorithms is hardly new, but they—like the media channels that employ them—have a new master. They no longer look predominantly for keywords or meta-tags; they are searching for and acting on *engagement by individuals,* and we marketers need to expand our idea of how, where, and when we optimize for organic experiences.

Traditionally we marketers have employed the long-standing practice of search engine optimization (SEO) to improve our brand's ranking in search results, and many of us still rely on it. This practice of building web experiences to meet the criteria that search engines seek has led us to busily fret over keywords, meta-tags, page load times, and dozens of other factors. The ranking algorithm used by major search engines still demands that we keep to the general rules of SEO, but that is not sufficient to get our brand experiences to show up on page one of search results. We now must also focus on interaction with our audience.

This same focus on interaction applies to social news feeds as well. When news feeds started out, they were chronological accounts of our networks; now they are contextual accounts. To see what I mean, take a look at your news feed on Facebook, and note the date and time the posts were created. You'll notice a wide range: some were created moments before, some years before. They are showing up in your feed based not on chronology but on contextual engagement. And the most important form of engagement is an interaction—a comment, conversation, share, or like. When a person or brand is able to drive interaction with an experience, it becomes more likely to be shown to others (as we saw with "the mention"), spreading the experience farther and farther. So what determines a post's reach is not its publication but rather people's participation with it. In fact, interaction drives the organic availability of brand experiences and content in all settings. Retailers such as Amazon and Apple's App Store operate the same way. They look for engagement with items to help them filter through thousands of products, which enables these retailers to make the best recommendations possible to their users.

To be clear, interaction is just one of many factors driving algorithms (some of which are brands' highly guarded secrets), but it is the major one, coupled with SEO, that allows marketers some ability to make their brand experiences available to the people expressly looking for them.

An outstanding example of participation now being more powerful than publication occurred the day after the 2016 US presidential election. That day, if you searched for "election results" on your browser, the number one search result was not CNN or any of the major news outlets; it was the website 70news.wordpress.com. That's right, a website hosted on a free domain hacked the biggest news story of the decade, because, based on the engagement it was able to create with its election story, the search algorithms determined 70news would provide the best experience for its users.

How did 70news.wordpress.com do it? It used a set of tactics to drive engagement that included salacious headlines and memes designed to emotionally connect with its right-wing audience. These memes and headlines, shared across social media, email, and other third-party news sites, homed in on exactly what they knew their audience wanted to see and share.

We all share stories, posts, and memes that validate the image we hold of ourselves. 70news's audience was primarily far-right-leaning people, so when they were presented with a story or meme that validated their position, they readily interacted with it, often without ever reading the underlying story. (By the way, this isn't just a right-wing thing; a Columbia University study found that 60 percent of articles shared on social media are not read by the person sharing the article.[9]) Each of these shares, likes, or comments on the 70news story became another engagement, signaling to the algorithm that it likely would be engaging to others, driving up its organic reach.

But here's the key to why 70news climbed to the top: CNN.com's official election results page included 82 backlinks (other sites referencing your content as the source of their story) and 40,000 social shares. But the news story on 70news had 1,500 backlinks and more than 400,000 social shares. So even though CNN had been online decades longer and had a much larger total presence and a larger social following, it lost out in search results to a small player, strictly because in the infinite era *algorithms favor participation* over publication.

This phenomenon was made possible by the fact that people on social media trust what they find more than they should (though that is now changing). It's also likely that some of this engagement was driven by a new and nefarious tactic: bot armies. These armies of artificially intelligent bots can be programmed to respond as a provocative troll in the comments section of various platforms to spur conversation and controversy. And, of course, people find controversy engaging—and engagement makes content more available organically.

By no means am I suggesting that you create fake news or engage in black hat tactics such as bot armies. I offer this example to show that getting your audience to interact with your content is paramount to being organically available. Simply publishing and promoting content is not enough. To be available in any of these search results or news feeds, brands need to add targeted engagement with social media and other sites to their daily to-do lists. We marketers need to expand our vision and consider the many questions and conversations that potentially take place over the life cycle of every customer. Most of the questions you can answer and the conversations you can join best occur on sites other than our own, because they offer greater context to our audiences.

For example, marketers at Acquia, an open source software company, noticed a question posted to Quora (a social question-and-answer portal) that they knew their prospective buyers were asking along their journey. Rather than answer the question "as a brand," it leveraged advocates to answer it for them by posting a link to the Quora question in its community portal. More than twenty of its brand advocates added comments to the Quora post directly, each from their personal account, adding their own personal story. These advocates willingly spent their time answering the question and advocating for Acquia (that's the power of advocacy, the final step in the new customer journey that we'll explore more in part three). Most important, because of the engagement those advocates drove to the Quora post, it is now the number one result for that particular question and is continually being served up to each new person who asks it. In creating this cycle, Acquia leveraged the value it had already created for its customers to reach more people and guide them toward its brand in a highly contextual way.

This strategy of leveraging other channels to ensure that your brand surfaces organically also applies to traditional public relations efforts, such as narrative control. Where traditional PR is about publishing a story in the media to control the narrative of the moment, PR should also be looking to control narrative along the customer journey by answering the questions marketing has identified and working to land story lines specifically for SEO. Marketing, in fact, should work closely with PR teams because a brand's site does not have the same power as a publication.

For example, it would be hard for a brand's website to rank in a Google search for the term "best looks for fall," but it wouldn't be hard for your PR team to pitch a story to a powerfully ranked publication to get your brand name listed in an article about it. Once the story is live, context marketers can motivate their audience to interact with the article, driving the story higher on the page of search results. When your brand is available on that page in the moment someone is looking for it, you have made your brand experience organic in the most powerful context possible.

Looking at the three major ways described in this chapter to make your brand experiences available, one theme carries through: the importance of interaction. Whether engaging audiences by email, through social media, or via a search engine, all channels are tuned to a new master that makes interaction more powerful than publication alone. In other words, yes, you need good content, but that is only the tip of the iceberg. The real work is interaction with individual members of your audience.

Now, let's look at the next element of context: creating brand experiences that are permissioned.

5.

Permissioned

Coordinating with Individuals to Give Them What They've Asked for, on Their Terms

Take a look at your inbox: there's almost nothing, not even in a promotions tab, that was directly delivered to you without some sort of permission granted by you (wittingly or not). The second element of the context framework, permission is a power all consumers now have that gives them control over who has access to them directly. It is a mechanism—which ranges from checking a box to providing personal data—by which an individual actively chooses to receive communication from a brand or its representative.

People use permission to further customize what they see on their screens each day, and to cut through the tremendous noise of the infinite era. Breaking through and driving interactions that will make your brand available in the two most efficient ways (direct or organic), as described in the last chapter, requires permission. It's the foundation for reaching higher levels of context, and consumers grant it in one of two forms.

Permission Is Either Implicit or Explicit

Permission is not new; it is something marketers have focused on since Seth Godin's breakout book in 1999, *Permission Marketing*. In his best seller, Godin focuses on the notion of permission via email. While email remains important, in the infinite media era there's a wide range of permissions we marketers must seek.

Like the other four elements in the framework, permission levels lie along a continuum. Implicit permission sits closest to the center as least contextual (see figure 5-1), and explicit permission lies at the outer edge—the highest level of context, expressly granted by an individual and most desired by marketers. When you lack permission to communicate with users of a media channel, your brand experiences are tantamount to forced ads, which as we learned in chapter 4 have very little context, if any.

FIGURE 5-1

The context framework (permissioned)

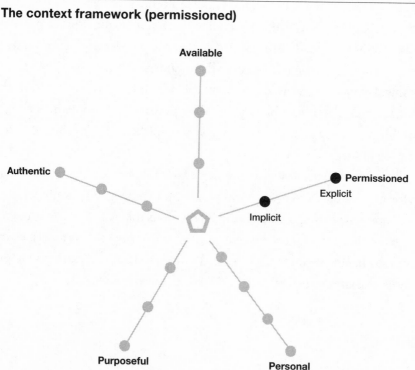

People grant implicit permission when they engage with your brand before you've reached out to them. For example, a person who visits your site is implicitly allowing you to access his or her personal data to create a more personal experience, although the person is not actively giving you permission to reach out to him or her on another channel. Consumers are aware you are tracking them, and an Accenture study found 83 percent of retail consumers are happy to passively share personal data that allows brands to create a better experience for them.[1]

Traditionally, brands are implicitly able to access one of three kinds of data: first-, second-, or third-party data. First-party data is any data the brand owns, which could be created in a host of ways. It could be browsing history created by the individual while on the website, information the individual shared in a form, or past purchasing history. Second-party data is someone else's first-party data that the brand buys to augment its own data, allowing the brand to create richer experiences. Finally, there is third-party data, typically purchased from a large data provider or data exchange. These exchanges combine a mass amount of data from many sources to show a more complete picture of each consumer. The data isn't able to identify a person by name, but it could tell you that the person on your website right now is forty-five, from Texas, and an avid golfer looking to buy an SUV in the next sixty days. All three data types are passively created and do not require the individual to take action for the data to be generated. Many consumers don't mind allowing brands to collect and use this data because it is leveraged to create a better experience *in that moment*. That's the major difference between implicit and explicit permission. Implicit permission grants a brand the ability to use personal data in the moment, but it does not parlay to direct outreach; for that you need explicit permission, which allows continuous communication and a greater range of context to be created across channels. Explicit permission can be granted in different ways too. Individuals could give you their email addresses when filling out a form and checking a box that it is OK to communicate with them via the channel. On social media, "liking" your brand or giving it a "follow" does the same.

Explicit permission also provides brands with reliable reach. When an individual gives a brand or its representative explicit permission to communicate, you've upped the context of your relationship considerably, and your chances of getting your brand experience through are almost guaranteed. Direct messages on channels such as email and Facebook Messenger are reliable, although they might be placed in a separate folder. Such messages are definitely more reliable for getting your experience delivered than posting on social media, which has only a 1 percent reach. But there's one other big key that context marketers should focus on when it comes to using explicit permission: direct engagement via social channels. The power of social media isn't free publication; it's personal connection. Each person has the ability to directly engage with anyone else, and as brands we must learn to embrace this. Mass publication was where we came from—personal connection is the way forward.

Brand experiences on social media are seen by only a very small portion of your followers because of the sheer number of media circulating in the infinite era. (This is likely the reason there are no more "Like Us on Facebook" signs littering the landscape.) Gaining a following is still important, but more important is that your marketing department gain explicit permission to engage with individuals, providing your brand with reliable reach. This is the new frontier of marketing, and it's how brands are able to reach higher levels of context in the lives of their customers and soon-to-be customers.

Such individual interactions might sound way too granular or intrusive, but they are 100 percent reliable and provide deep value to the consumer. Consumers do want engagement on social channels, but not from random brands. So although your brand doesn't have to get permission to engage with an individual on social media, it would be out of context (and likely unwelcome) to do so if you don't have that individual's permission. Once you have permission, it is acceptable to engage. And of course your direct interactions on social media go beyond just that individual, giving your brand exposure to the person's followers and connections. These kinds of direct engagements also become key signals to the AI driving the cycle of context forward.

Without permission of some kind, whether it's explicit or implicit, the brand experience is forced, just like a magazine ad is forced. The consumer is not asking for the "moment"; you have forced the entire thing on him or

FIGURE 5-2

Personal data increases context

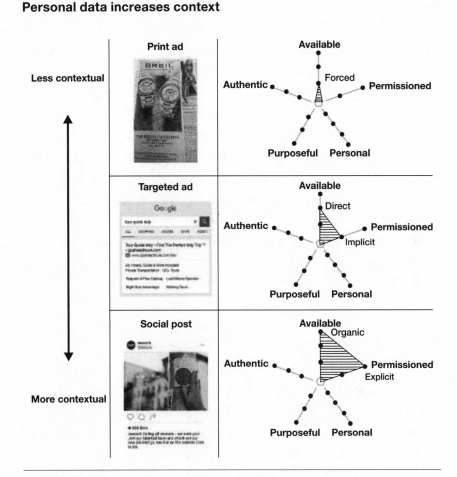

her. But if we as brands are able to meet consumers in *their* moments, they will be willing to passively share information with us and grant us implicit permission to leverage personal data to create a better experience for them in that moment. Figure 5-2 illustrates how personal data is used to create a more contextual organic experience.

Driving engagement after you've received permission will still depend on how well you use the other four elements of the context framework to make that experience contextual *to the moment*. But getting consumers' explicit permission is what opens those doors.

Brands Must Work to Gain Explicit Permission

As I already noted, things are very different today than in 1999 when Seth Godin first proposed the idea of gaining permission. But while the processes we use today have changed, the same basic idea applies: a brand offers an experience that's so great that people actively want to follow it, or else the brand must ask for permission. As you progress with context marketing and your brand experiences reach a larger audience, you will naturally gain new followers, but don't rely on organic growth alone. You'll need to learn how to grow your audience, and the only way to do that is to ask.

But given the infinite changes in the media environment, how should we go about asking for permission today? Let's look at two keys to gaining explicit permission in our modern time: the "follow first" and the value exchange.

Follow First

When you're trying to gain permission, here's a winning formula: find the followers you wish were already following your brand, and follow them. It sounds simple, but many brands still resist this very basic approach because they overestimate their organic reach and underestimate the ego of humans.

Brands still believe they will gain followers organically, based simply on the content they produce. And that may well be true, but only if your brand already has millions of followers and drives massive engagement. That's not the reality for many brands on social media, and certainly not where they start out. If you are starting out today, the best way is to first identify your core audience. There are many tools to help you filter through the data available on social media to find people who are a natural fit. For example, you may track a hashtag and filter all users of that tag to a specific geography.

If you are a boutique hotel, for example, you might search for #beststay to find people to follow who posted about their hotel stay while on vacation or doing business (even if they didn't post about your hotel—yet). And remember, your audience is more than just potential customers; it should include the influencers in your business, your partners, and other individuals and brands active in your space. That's your audience, and sometimes they are easily found with a search. But often you'll have to do a bit more digging to find them.

Beyond using simple keywords to search, you could find brands or individuals with a large audience and work your way through their followers, or else rely on tools and AI to suggest people for you. However you find them, the next step is the same: simply request to follow them. Each channel calls this action something different; LinkedIn calls it "connecting," while Instagram calls it "following." People love it when others want to follow them. Remember, they are on social media for a reason; following a person constitutes validation that what he or she is doing is loved, wanted, and relevant. Once someone has accepted your request, you are immediately available for private messages and direct communications and able to engage with the person's content in a contextual way.

Before you begin following people, you should plan ahead and think through the action. For example, if your brand is new to people, you should expect them to look at your social profile as a part of their evaluation. They are unlikely to give you permission if they notice your social feed is a giant ad campaign. You're going to have to prepare your accounts to fit the value you're trying to deliver. Make sure your bio, posts, and engagement are all up to par and able to show the value of people following you back.

Offer a Value Exchange

Nearly every retail-clothing site offers visitors a percentage discount off their first online order in exchange for the visitor's personal email address. That's a value exchange, and it grants permission for the brand to deliver experiences and interact with that customer directly. Even though subsequent emails from that retailer have a good chance of going to the customer's spam folder (or its cousin, Gmail's promotions tab), collecting email addresses is still important. It provides a gateway to gaining more information and greater context—eventually.

For example, many professional services or B2B companies develop content marketing so that they have something of value to exchange for a

FIGURE 5-3

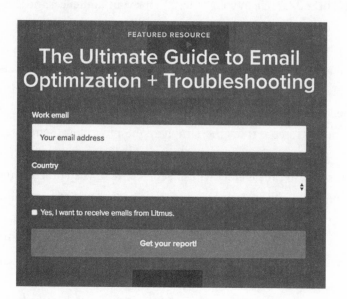

Source: Litmus website.

prospect's email address and other information. People have come to expect such offers when researching services that cater to certain industries,
such as business consulting, cybersecurity, financial services, and so on.
In figure 5-3, the email marketing tool Litmus asks prospects to check the
box "Yes, I want to receive emails from Litmus" to gain explicit permission to contact them beyond the delivery of its "Ultimate Guide."

If a prospect doesn't check the box, Litmus does not have explicit permission to send emails beyond delivering the "Ultimate Guide" report.
Does that mean it technically can't email the person? No, it means Litmus
does not have explicit permission. One could argue it has implicit permission, but because Litmus *asked* the prospect for explicit permission, using
that email address to send other material risks irritating or even angering
the prospect. Such an action by a brand communicates a lack of integrity.

The value exchange also works on social media channels. On LinkedIn,
for example, HubSpot created a central meeting place for like-minded marketing professionals by assembling a "Group" of LinkedIn members focused on inbound marketing. In exchange for membership, HubSpot

provides thought-leadership content that educates the group on how to be better marketers, and the company curates conversations on marketing topics that help members achieve their business goals. Each of these pieces of content and every conversation also directly helps HubSpot, since it is teaching its audience new ways of marketing that also leverage its tool, thus creating demand without ever creating ads.

The Inbound Marketing Group has grown rapidly because of the value that HubSpot offers in exchange for membership. Early on, HubSpot organized and moderated events associated with the group, but soon the roles reversed, and the group itself began to create the majority of the content and conversation. In 2015, HubSpot's Inbound Marketing Group proved key to the brand's achieving the world record for the largest webinar ever held (a new category created by HubSpot's record)—with 31,100 registrants.[2] But it all began with HubSpot seeking permission through a value exchange offered to highly engaged LinkedIn members in a contextual way.

When creating a value exchange on a social media platform, be sure you match your content to the expectations of people using the platform. It makes sense for HubSpot to offer thought leadership to attract members to its Inbound Marketing Group on LinkedIn, because people often search LinkedIn for people and content related to their profession. But how would that content play on a platform such as Facebook? Not well. But that doesn't mean B2B brands should skip the more purely social platforms. Brands should embrace the many channels their customers are on, but make sure they shift how they use them to match the value the consumers are seeking on each channel.

Kronos, an enterprise brand, uses Facebook to break through to new audiences with its #timewellspent cartoon series. Instead of focusing on its service offering, Kronos offers the Facebook audience something congruent with their reason for spending time on the platform: to escape, laugh, and share funny content with their friends and followers. On average, each of these comics drives upward of 300 likes, shares, and comments, which builds Kronos's following. In fact, Kronos's Facebook followers have proven to like only the comics: there's a stark drop in engagement with the corporate blog posts Kronos published on Facebook. For example, three recent Kronos comics combined generated more than 1,057 likes, comments, and shares, while Kronos's three recent corporate blogs drove only a total of 16 likes, no shares, and no comments. That makes its comics more than sixty times more likely to break through. This doesn't mean that Kronos can't find a way to reach followers with its service and industry-oriented content; it just means it needs to do so using the right channel. And the company will more likely break through in other channels by having already gained recognition and following on Facebook. The long and short of it is that you shouldn't try to do everything in one channel. Connect with your audience with content that suits each channel, and stick with it.

Once permission has been granted—either implicitly by someone visiting your website or explicitly by someone filling out a form, conversing with a chatbot, or following your brand—your company can gain access to the individual's personal data, which will become the fuel powering your contextual efforts going forward.

Explicit Permission Grants Access to Better Data

As I've noted, consumers grant implicit permission with relative ease. In the United States, the moment someone visits your website or other owned media channels, you have implicit permission to track that individual's personal behavior across your website, and most consumers are happy to let this happen. This might change, however, should the United States decide to follow the European Union model, in which companies are not allowed to track the personal data of individuals without explicit permission. Hence, the pop-up on Britain's *Financial Times* site (see figure 5-4).

But as the continuum illustrates, having implicit permission is only the beginning; explicit permission can improve the data you're able to access. While implicit permission gives you information about consumer behavior, remember that data isn't perfect. Just because a consumer looks at a product doesn't mean she or he wants to buy it. To gather the best data, therefore, brands need to ask consumers for data directly, gaining explicit permission to use it. The better the data, the greater the potential context we can reach and the richer the personal brand experiences we can offer— topics we'll explore in the next chapter. We might get such data from a

FIGURE 5-4

Source: https://www.ft.com/.

survey or form, or an email preference center in which they state what content they want. Personal data will be smaller in volume than the behavioral data we collect, but it provides two major benefits to brand: it's regulation-proof, and it provides clear guidelines for context.

To access explicitly permissioned data, you must do four things. First, ask for it, via a form, a chatbot, or even from a live conversation with a representative of your brand. Second, explain how you plan to use the data. Salesforce research found 86 percent of consumers trust a brand more with their data if the brand reps explain how the data will be used. The *Financial Times* did a good job of this, stating clearly how the company is going to use your data. Third, be transparent about how you are using personal data. At any point if an individual were to ask, "Why am I seeing this?" the brand should be able to provide the data driving that decision. Fourth, allow consumers to see what data you have on them and allow them to turn it on, or off, and even amend it if they like. The same Salesforce research found that 92 percent of customers trust brands with their data when the brand gives them control over it.[3]

When brands take these four steps to gain explicit permission, they not only foster trust among their customers but also create a reliable flow of personal data that is regulation-proof. But beyond that, such permission provides powerful guard rails for context. For example, asking people if you can email them is seeking "permission," but going a step further to ask "What types of emails would you like?" is better. The answer will guide your email programs, helping you increase the context of your direct communications by sending only the type of content consumers prefer. Do they only want to receive coupons, your newsletter, or both? Let them tell you.

Such personal data will also help you keep customers moving through their journey. Asking how satisfied customers are (for example, emailing out a customer satisfaction survey) provides you with detailed explicit data about how to continue forward. If they aren't happy, you need to pull back, evaluate what you're doing, and fix whatever the problem is. If they are happy, maybe you automate a program inviting them to become an advocate. The explicitly permissioned data you've gained is what drives such programs, and you can gain that permission only if you ask.

––––––––––

Permission is a key element of context. All of your future efforts will hinge on the personal data your brand can access once it has permission. Without permission, you will be unable to reach higher context in the experiences you offer customers. Brands following the four steps I outlined in this chapter will always be able to access personal data and use it to grow trust and improve the context of any moment.

Next we'll look at how we use that data to make moments and experiences more personal—the next element in the context framework.

6.

Personal

Going Beyond How Personal the Experience Is to How Personally You Can Deliver It

Every moment in the infinite media environment is personal, and no two moments are ever the same. Your mobile device is set to your specific preferences and displays an array of apps chosen by you. Every media channel you visit filters tens of thousands of experiences down to a handful, just for you. Your entire relationship with media is recorded in your every action—from which the environment infers your desires—allowing it to serve you increasingly personal experiences in increasingly relevant and meaningful context.

In other words, delivering your brand's experience in a personal way, the third element of our context framework, has become the new baseline for motivating modern consumers. Personal goes far beyond superficial personalization of content (which has been around for decades—think of mass mailers addressed to you personally or mass emails that start with a personal greeting that includes your name). Rather, it builds on the other elements of the framework to meet individuals in your audience where they are—in the moment—reaching a deeper personal connection.

As with the other elements, there's a continuum of how personal you can make your brand experience (see figure 6-1). *Mass campaigns* are the least

FIGURE 6-1

The context framework (personal)

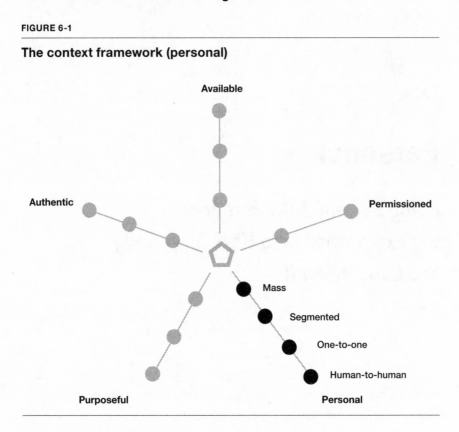

personal/contextual because the brand experience is public and reaches everyone in the same way. A bit more personal is *segmentation*, in which you tailor your brand experience to a smaller group of some kind, making it more useful to those specific people.

One-to-one efforts are more personal still, because your brand has crafted an experience for a single person, customized to match the person's needs at a specific moment. Such experiences are very contextual, but because they're still conducted between a brand and a person, they don't reach the apex of what the personal element can deliver: *human-to-human* interaction. This most contextual level on the personal continuum involves direct contact, where the experience is not only unique but also delivered by one human to another—usually brand employees, brand advocates, or members of social or other communities, all working on a brand's behalf. Let's look at each of those levels more closely.

Mass Campaigns

At the lowest point on the continuum, mass campaigns are familiar to us all: making a brand experience available in a way that will reach as many people as possible with a single act. That might mean anything from a billboard ad to a TV spot on a cable channel to an email blast sent to an enormous list of names. In the golden age of advertising, during the limited media era, mass campaigns were the way—the only way—advertisers reached customers, through the media channels of that time. While outdated now, those methods were highly effective at the time. Many of the most acclaimed marketing campaigns of all time were created via mass media, such as the Think Small campaign, which launched the VW Beetle into the hearts of Americans and made it the best-selling car ever (at that time, which was 1972).[1] The entire campaign was mass media.

Today mass campaigns rarely motivate consumers, for all the reasons we've discussed about how the infinite media era works: consumers can ask any question and receive a trusted answer in an instant, thereby killing the power of forced messages to drive consumer behavior. But even though consumers have found a better way to operate today, mass campaigns to distribute brand experiences can easily become more contextual. They just need to use a basic *segmentation*, the next level up the continuum of the personal element. The delivery works much the same as with mass campaigns, except the experience goes to smaller groups and uses some basic personalization in the message.

For example, you could hire an influencer on social media to message his or her entire audience a uniform communication about your brand. That would make your mass campaign at least permissioned (explicitly) and available (directly), between influencer and audience. In the context framework, that campaign would begin to look like what we see in figure 6-2.

FIGURE 6-2

Plotting the elements of available, permissioned, and personal

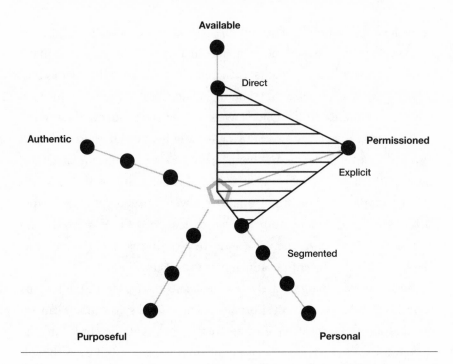

Segmentation

Moving up the continuum of the personal element from mass campaigns that marketers deliver in a segmented way, we arrive at the fullest expression of segmentation. Like mass campaigns, segmentation is also well known to marketers. We segment brand experiences by tailoring them to a smaller geography, interest, or activity. This makes the experience more useful to that group, increasing the likelihood of engagement. For example, Spartan Race, an organization that creates obstacle course–based running races, segments its email list by geography. The messaging in the emails changes based on the subscriber's location, with an aim to increase the number of registrants at every race. I live in the southern United States, and as someone who has raced in a Spartan Race in the past, I receive information about races in cities near me. Segmenting is a great way to

FIGURE 6-3

**Increased context by expanding the available
and personal elements**

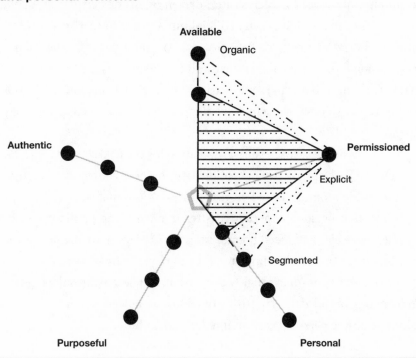

improve how relevant your context becomes, especially if you even slightly tailor your message to the more targeted group. It's not wildly personal, but definitely more contextual, as shown in figure 6-3.

One-to-one

Reaching a still greater level of context are one-to-one brand experiences. These are created by the brand and delivered to a single person at a single moment. While well understood in theory, such experiences are much less common in practice because of the technical requirements to carry them off. One-to-one is a true tool of the infinite media era. Here's how it works: marketers combine an individual's personal data with technology that allows them to precisely customize the brand experience, content, channel, timing, and delivery. Recall the example from part one of the furniture brand Room & Board. The company designed its website to fluidly create a unique experience for each visitor, driven by his or her personal data. Room & Board also leveraged artificial intelligence to further contextualize its brand experience. The AI captures and analyzes—via implicit permission—the behavior of visitors to the site, instantly using that data to create a hyperpersonal experience for each person. Note that this level of one-to-one can only happen with advanced technology, specifically AI.

Similarly, ServiceMax, a software solution for the field service reps from GE Digital, uses predictive AI to identify the best content for each site visitor, in the moment, based on real-time data automatically gathered to optimize that person's experience. After implementing predictive AI on its site, ServiceMax reduced bounce rates by 70 percent, increased conversions by three times, and upped total demo requests by six times.

No doubt, one-to-one is highly contextual. But because it is the faceless, amorphous brand delivering the content, it is not as contextual as the ultimate on the personal continuum: human-to-human.

Human-to-human

Human-to-human experiences break through not because they are personalized but because *they are delivered personally*. Backcountry, an online outdoor retailer, offers a great example of this most contextual personal experience. Backcountry's website creates personal experiences through content that is dynamic and predictive. For example, if you are searching for a camp shoe, the site will include in its results some other products that people like you have "ultimately purchased" or "also viewed." A personal note written about the product by the user community will also appear (see figure 6-4).

So the website effectively predicts the products you want based on the actions of other purchasers just like you. Moreover, there are numerous reviews of each product from the Backcountry community, and live chat is there to help customers in real time. But the personal experience doesn't

FIGURE 6-4

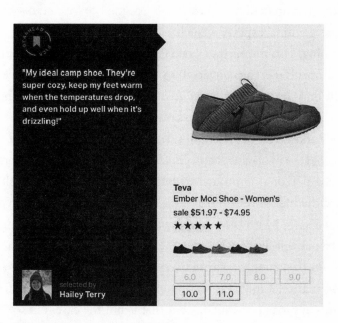

Source: https://www.backcountry.com/rc/gearhead-picks.

end there. Backcountry is capable of reaching every customer, human-to-human, with its Gearhead program, which I experienced myself.

A few days after I bought some snowboarding gear on the Backcountry site for an upcoming trip, I received a phone call from Wesley, a "Gearhead." He was calling to ask if I had any questions about my new gear or if I wanted to chat about snowboarding. I told him about my upcoming trip, and I genuinely enjoyed our brief conversation. Later that day I received a personal email from Wesley as a follow-up. The sole purpose of all the communication was summed up in this one line of his email: "Whether you have issues with returns, want to place an order, or just want to call up to chat about some gear for an upcoming trip, I am available."

To be clear, Wesley was not trying to sell me more stuff (not directly); rather, he was looking to build a personal, lasting relationship. After this amazingly effective encounter, I looked more deeply into the Gearhead program. Backcountry employs 150 Gearheads, whose responsibilities range from managing larger accounts to overseeing the online chat and, of course, direct customer engagement. What makes this program different from others I've researched? Gearheads are assigned to an activity in which they have genuine expertise, such as mountain biking, snowboarding, and climbing. This means that when Gearheads reach out to customers, as Wesley did with me, the conversation is engaging and substantive. Someone with only textbook knowledge of a sport like snowboarding is not going to be able to converse at the same level.

Chris Purkey, vice president of sales and customer experience at Backcountry, told the magazine *Retail TouchPoints* that the Gearhead program's direct and personal approach to building customer relationships has increased the lifetime customer value of those customers 40 percent over those not engaged with the program, and it has increased ordering behavior by 105 percent. Purkey believes the program will drive $100 million of business for Backcountry within two years.[2]

At first glance, it might seem that involving the human hand (or voice) makes this approach unscalable, but that is not the case. Purkey believes that without automation, a Gearhead staff member is limited to managing only two hundred customers at a time. It simply is too time-consuming to know who to reach out to, what to talk about, and when. Managing even such a small set of customers would be a full-time role without technology. But with the correct technology, this personal outreach could easily scale to ten thousand customers, each in a human-to-human way because the technology can guide the Gearhead to the correct conversation to be had, at the correct moment. (More on how to apply automation in part three.)

Backcountry is one of those rare high performers that have *changed their idea of marketing* by aspiring to the most contextual goal on the personal continuum: human-to-human brand experiences. The result? Its marketing department has created a sales force whose explicit goal isn't to sell more product but rather to build relationships and aid consumers. That in turn adds significantly to the bottom line.

Some brands don't need to change their idea of marketing; they start out with contextual practices and never look back. That's what Mark Organ, marketing visionary and cofounder of Eloqua and current CEO of Influitive, told me in a recent conversation for this book. Organ says he's seen many newly launched brands forgo making traditional marketing hires in their early stages. Instead, they hire "community managers," who specialize in developing individual relationships with targeted audiences and customers to jump-start results. This very personal, direct engagement gives those early-stage brands two very powerful things: direct access to key influencers in the community, and a platform they can then leverage to drive up the context of their future efforts. Later, once they have their community going, they bring on the additional experience of SEO, email marketing, and so on, leveraging their community—not force—to extend the reach of their efforts.

The role of the community manager changes, depending on the specific organization. But generally it's someone who is actively managing and growing the community. The key is to think of community managers as coaches and the members as teammates. The coach is always recruiting, organizing, and working directly with each player to accomplish a goal. The focus isn't on the coach but on the players. This same analogy should hold with the experiences you're asking your community to share. The brand (coach) should be in the background, with the focus on common connection shared by the community.

This topic of a brand's community goes deeper than your standard subscribers, fans, and followers. Community not only defines an effective part of human-to-human brand experience; it also represents one of the starkest differences between traditional and context marketing. Let's look at it more closely.

Making Things Personal Through Your Brand Community

Ultimately, all brands need to move toward a more distributed community model. Call those communities social influencer programs, employee advocacy groups, and brand ambassadors. They all mean essentially the same thing: people, whether employees, social influencers, or brand advocates, who take actions to promote your brand by using their own personal social channels.

Why are such communities so critical to context marketing? They open exponentially more doors to human-to-human contact through each community member's own list of friends, followers, and the like, and each member's personal connection to their audience makes it more likely that the experience will break through, far more so than if the brand tried to break in from outside the community. Additionally, when multiple people begin to share an experience, the combination engagement signals the AI, increasing the total reach. The combined audience of such advocates and influencers is likely far bigger than your brand's, making your brand experience infinitely more contextual. Even more important: the deeply developed relationships that these community members have with their followers allows your brand to immediately benefit from the trust those people have built with their audiences over time. That's the power of brand advocates.

Brand Advocates and Their Superpowers

Brand advocates are a very powerful tool that marketers now have at their disposal. Remember, in the infinite era, everyone can create media, so rather than compete with that content, brands need to find ways to leverage it. At Salesforce, we have created a team of Salesforce customer MVPs who love the brand so much, they have become brand advocates. They help Salesforce create greater community and strengthen the bond between our brand and our customers. MVPs support the Salesforce Trailhead program, an education platform where individuals (not just customers but anyone who wants the training) can join, learn, and improve their careers by posting better results using our technology. Participants earn "badges" for completing courses on a wide range of topics, from how to begin using the Salesforce technology to best practices in sales, service, and marketing.

When Jonathon gained a new badge as part of Salesforce's Trailhead community, he shared the news on LinkedIn (see figure 6-5). Salesforce liked his post, and so did Becka, a Salesforce MVP. Because her comment on his post is human-to-human, it carries more weight and also reflects well on the Salesforce brand. That's how brand advocates like the MVPs at Salesforce take actions on a brand's behalf to strengthen relationships

FIGURE 6-5

Source: Author's LinkedIn feed.

with customers and extend the brand, human-to-human, in highly contextual ways.

Here's another example. SocialChorus, a social marketing technology company, found that a firm's employees have on average ten times more social connections than does the brand itself. Tesla, for example, has a little more than two million followers, while Elon Musk, its CEO, has more than twenty-two million followers. Many companies have a number of high-level staff with a strong following on a variety of social media platforms, but even the smaller followings of regular employees can be very powerful brand extenders, allowing your human-to-human efforts to scale. The math works out that leveraging 135 employees' social handles to share brand experiences creates the same impact as a single brand audience 1,000,000 people strong.[3] Considering the average B2B brand has a social following of only 50,000, using the same math, it would take only six people to reach an audience of the same size.

Many companies will enlist associates from several departments to promote relevant brand experiences (for example, your IT people would promote technology-related experiences and conferences). But at a minimum, all marketing and sales people should be using some of their time to share and engage with posts on behalf of your brand, as well as comment on and share content posted by related brands, industry leaders, and members of your brand audience. That is the kind of activity that increases your brand's human-to-human interactions—and the overall context of your brand experiences.

Sales teams can take enormous leaps forward by becoming brand advocates and using human-to-human brand experiences to create the connections that move leads along the customer journey. This is commonly referred to as *social selling*. In fact, AT&T used human-to-human experiences as its primary method for breaking into new accounts, reaching key prospects through a combination of targeted social media conversations and content sharing. The AT&T sales team began by researching the social media presence of key prospects as well as the industry professionals those prospects would be interested in following, specifically on Twitter and LinkedIn. The team used the "follow first" method described in an earlier chapter and joined the same groups as these people, multiplying their potential ways to connect by commenting on similar threads and, perhaps, joining the same conversations about the issues that matter to their prospects.

Again, keeping the brand in the background is absolutely crucial to the success of human-to-human contextual marketing. So when AT&T salespeople interacted with prospects and industry leaders, they were not at all "salesy" in their comments or questions. Communicating from their own (permissioned) social handles, they engaged in social media messaging, mentioned key prospects in the threads of relevant posts, shared content directly or with entire groups, and congratulated prospects on business awards—staying focused on the conversations that matter to their prospects and the industry, not necessarily to AT&T. The cumulative effect of this activity was the creation of multiple human-to-human relationships that are very difficult to create through phone calls and email. Why? Because *cold calls have no context*. Phone calls are valuable, as Wesley proved earlier, but only work when there is sufficient context. Cold calls are devoid of context, but a follow-up from a purchase isn't. Moreover, people are not interested in giving their time and attention to "a brand," but they might to a person—as I did to the Gearhead who contacted me. That distinction is important: the AT&T engagements that occurred were not with AT&T the brand but rather with a person who happens to work there.

Referring to this contextual effort, an AT&T employee reports: "By asking specific questions related to the content and by mentioning specific customers and people of interest on Twitter, we received engagement from customers, who began to ask questions or agree or challenge points we made in the blogs . . . They told us our approach was 'refreshing' because we were building relationships without bombarding them with sales calls, emails, and meetings" (as the competition was doing). This tactic of identifying a community first, and actively becoming a part of it through human-to-human experiences, is the apex of the personal element repertoire—and it landed AT&T a total of more than $40 million in new business, directly from this effort.[4]

Once your brand experience breaks through, because you've made it personal as well as available and permissioned, the final two elements of context—authentic and purposeful—will determine how your brand is received and whether your audience will interact with it. In other words, the final two elements of the context framework are the ones that determine its success in the end. Much more than mere final touches, they are the heart and soul of the context revolution. The next chapter explores the element of authentic.

7.

Authentic

Combining Voice, Empathy, and Channel Congruence Simultaneously

Authentic is easily the most subjective element of the context framework. Everyone has a different idea about what makes a communication authentic or not. But get it wrong, and you'll pay a price. Even when your brand experience hits the most contextual levels of being available, permissioned, and personal, it will flop if it strikes an inauthentic note. Just ask Pepsi.

In a video ad featuring the model Kendall Jenner, Pepsi attempted to connect with its audience using a theme of social justice. As one of the biggest brands on the planet, Pepsi has at its disposal a cadre of ad agencies, which no doubt programmed the video as part of a coordinated campaign, from paid media to influencer marketing. Instead, the ad failed miserably and had to be pulled within days of its launch.

Pepsi didn't simply miss the mark—it was far worse than that. Viewers were outraged at the connection that Pepsi was making between its brand and US social justice movements. Audiences saw the video as co-opting current movements and protests, a cheap attempt to piggyback on the plight of others for corporate profit. It set off a firestorm of bad press, including a tweet from Bernice King, a daughter of Dr. Martin Luther King (see figure 7-1).

There is no brand out there that could work its way back from that level of inauthenticity. At first Pepsi defended the ad as promoting diverse people coming together in a "spirit of harmony." But within twenty-four hours of

FIGURE 7-1

Source: https://twitter.com/berniceking/status/849656699464056832?lang=en.

launching the ad, Pepsi pulled it and issued an apologetic message, stating that its attempt to "project a global message of unity . . . clearly missed the mark."[1]

But don't let this example make you believe that discerning what's authentic for your brand is always obvious. It's not at all. That's why it's so easy to get it wrong, sometimes very wrong. When you reach your audience with ever-more closely defined contextual experiences—having had individual buyers' permission to make those brand experiences available and personal, even human-to-human—the *quality* of your interactions becomes paramount. Everything else takes a back seat to delivering a high-quality, authentic experience. That means quality in consumers' interactions not just with your brand, service, and products but also with every person associated with your brand: internal brand ambassadors, service specialists, influencers, even your company leaders. In short, people expect brands to be more human and more *authentic* at every touchpoint. Nothing else matters as much.

But what, exactly, makes something authentic? We're all familiar with the basic meaning of authentic, especially as it refers to an object or artifact, such as a painting deemed genuine or original to a particular era or artist. Most of us also understand its meaning when we encounter other people. It's a way to describe their bearing and style. We say that someone is authentic when he or she acts in a way that we intuit as congruent with their inner selves. That type of judgment is a more subjective—and slippery—notion, yet it remains a clear level of discernment that people tend to agree on, one way or the other. That's the level of discernment we're talking about with the authentic element of context.

So how do we marketers make our brand experiences authentic, or congruent, with our brand values?

The Qualities of Authenticity

Given its subjective nature, the authentic element differs in an important way from the other elements in the context framework. Rather than lying on a continuum of higher and higher levels of authenticity that marketers can seek to achieve, it contains three qualities of equal value that combine to create the quality of authenticity: *voice, empathy,* and *alignment with the channel* in which you deliver the experience. Leverage any one of those qualities and your brand experience will be more contextual. But when all are present, the experience has the best chance to ring true and engage your audience on an authentic, human level (see figure 7-2).

Voice

We all know about the importance of establishing a brand voice. But how does voice change for brand experiences that engage consumers in close context? Simply put, it gets more conversational while still tracking to the core voice of your brand. For example, if you're a financial services brand, you might think that your voice should be strict and formal, justifying the buttoned-up tone by thinking people take money "seriously." While people

FIGURE 7-2

The context framework (authentic)

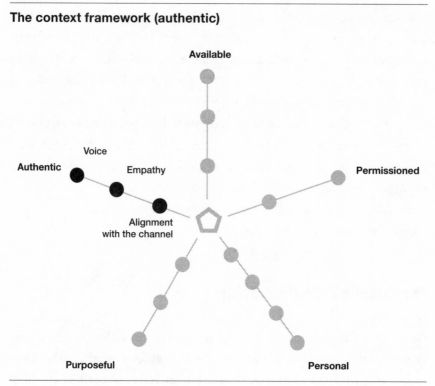

do take money seriously, the idea that these conversations have to be strict and formal isn't true. In a conversation with Joe Hyland, while he was CMO of the financial software company Taulia, he told me the company uses humor as a part of its voice "because all people laugh." Humans don't want a contrived brand voice; they want a human voice that uses the basic aspects of human conversation—natural language and dialogue.

Compare the following two brand experiences that I recently received through LinkedIn. Which do you find more engaging?

Message A:

Hi Mathew,

My name is XXXXXX and I'm a founding partner at the teen and young adult marketing agency, XXXXX.

WHAT WE DO

- Strategy, social media, creative, and experiential marketing services

- [AGENCY] is regularly cited as a "Best Place to Work" not only in [STATE], but by *Outside* magazine and others, so we attract the smartest, most hard-working people in marketing

- We never stop learning, working to improve, and educating our clients about youth culture; check out some of our recent white papers

- We work for *Fortune* 500 companies like Amazon, Pepsi, Dick's Sporting Goods, and others, but we also work for challengers, up-and-comers, and brands that are trying to connect with teens and young adults in an authentic way

- Since our founding in 1995, our client retention rate is 3.5x the industry average

If you think we provide the type of marketing that can be of service to you, please contact me.

Warmly,

XXXXXX

Message B:

"Hi Mathew, may I send you a copy of our marketing automation best practices guide? Based on some of your recent tweets, I thought you might be interested. Let me know (including which email address to send it to)! Many thanks, Shari"

The first message reads like a slide presentation, which makes the closing salutation, "Warmly," seem almost comical. The brand experience is completely inauthentic (despite using the word *authentic* in a bullet point), but it didn't need to be. By giving even minimal thought to the voice used (as well as making it empathic, as you will see momentarily), message A could have been transformed into an authentic human-to-human experience. For instance, the writer could have forgone the buzzwords and name-dropping in favor of using natural language, while trying to engage me in dialogue around a shared interest.

Message B, on the other hand, though brief (which often can be a plus), is much more authentic because it does those very things. The sender makes it known that she has done her homework by referring to a post I made on Twitter, she writes the note using colloquial language, and she opens up a dialogue around a shared topic. Which one do you think I responded to?

Empathy

Nobody cares about your brand. But they might begin to care, if you can prove you care about *them*. That's where empathy comes in, which is different from sympathy. Sympathy is about commiseration or pity in the face of someone else's misfortune or lot in life. Empathy goes a step further: it's about making an effort to view and understand things from another person's or group's perspective. When it comes to crafting authentic brand experiences, empathy is key.

That's especially true if you're trying to deliver an experience to the masses, such as the Pepsi video discussed at the beginning of this chapter. By nature, such mass dissemination is automatically less contextual, lying low on the personal continuum as we explored in an earlier chapter. But that doesn't mean such brand experiences can't be authentic.

Pepsi went wrong because it revealed a lack of empathy, even though, according to company statements, it was attempting to show it. But people saw the ad as decidedly nonempathic for a number of reasons, starting with the fact that Pepsi used staged protest imagery featuring a fashion model (Jenner) who had no activism experience. Then, toward the video's end, the ad clearly tried to evoke a photo that had gone viral (from a genuine protest after police killed Alton Sterling) of a young woman named Ieshia Evans facing down police in Baton Rouge, Louisiana. All that to sell soda.

Pepsi marketers hadn't paused to imagine what it would be like for huge portions of its audience to view the ad, and it proved an expensive, brand-damaging mistake. Not only did it get the sharp perspective of Dr. King's daughter, Bernice King, but it also received this tweet from DeRay Mckesson, an *actual* activist: "If I had carried a Pepsi I guess I never would've gotten arrested. Who knew?"

Being empathic when envisioning your brand experience won't just protect you from mistakes like Pepsi's. It's also a way for brands of all sizes to break through the noise and be remembered. We want to give our audiences what they desire, not just take up their time. That's how Wistia, a video hosting company, broke through in a big way with its marketing survey—perhaps the ultimate "hard sell." It did it by employing some empathy.

Most of us have sat around a conference table discussing how to create better content for our audience. The Wistia team was probably doing just that when it decided it would be more authentic to simply ask audience members what *they* really wanted to learn from a video hosting service. That required a survey, and the marketing staff honestly hated to ask its audience to do something they themselves would hate to do. Their empathic solution? To at least make their survey request entertaining, even if they couldn't make the survey itself very fun.

They decided to film a video in their offices, featuring a Wistia employee in the foreground and the rest of the team slightly out of focus in the background. The team member in focus begins by reading a short note laying out their conundrum: they want to make better content but need you, the viewer, to let them know what you want to learn. After she reads the note, she looks right into the camera and directly asks the audience to take the survey. Then the magic happens. The moment she finishes, she steps backward and fades into a dance line while the music rises and the entire company begins to dance the electric slide, singing in unison: "Duh, dun, dun, da, dun, dun, Take the Survey! Duh, dun, dun, da, dun, dun, Take the Survey!" The scene continues for a full minute and is completely delightful. Not only does it convey empathy for its audience, but it's also authentic to its brand, because it's a quirky video company that's using a quirky video to create the experience.

Wistia is a quirky brand, so the voice of the video is what its audience expects; still, the marketing department could only hope that it would land

FIGURE 7-3

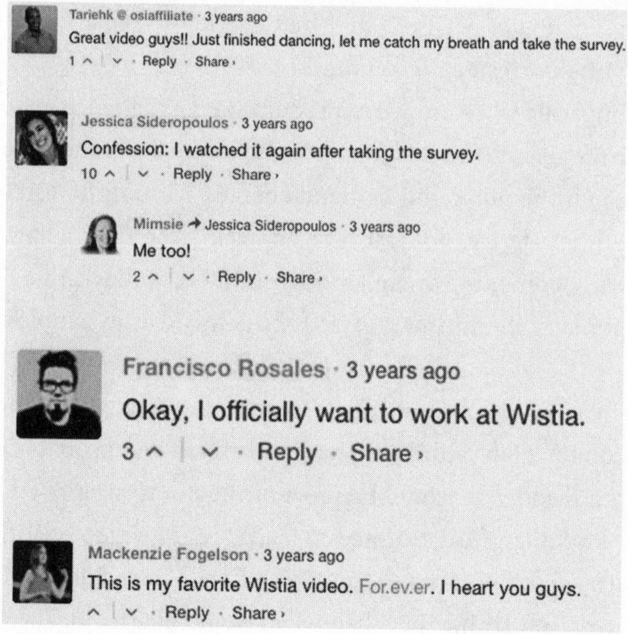

> Tariehk @ osiaffiliate · 3 years ago
> Great video guys!! Just finished dancing, let me catch my breath and take the survey.
> 1 ∧ ⌄ · Reply · Share ›
>
> Jessica Sideropoulos · 3 years ago
> Confession: I watched it again after taking the survey.
> 10 ∧ ⌄ · Reply · Share ›
>
>> Mimsie → Jessica Sideropoulos · 3 years ago
>> Me too!
>> 2 ∧ ⌄ · Reply · Share ›
>
> Francisco Rosales · 3 years ago
> Okay, I officially want to work at Wistia.
> 3 ∧ ⌄ · Reply · Share ›
>
> Mackenzie Fogelson · 3 years ago
> This is my favorite Wistia video. For.ev.er. I heart you guys.
> ∧ ⌄ · Reply · Share ›

Source: Wistia Learning Center Blog.

well with its audience. The response was beyond amazing. Not only did Wistia post the highest engagement rate of any survey it has ever run, but its audience members also connected with the company like they never had before (see figure 7-3).

In total, Wistia's survey-request post had forty-one comments, all with similar fanfare. Just imagine: you ask people to take a survey, and rather than pulling teeth to get them to do it, those people feel so engaged that they ask to work for your company.

Similarly, Southwest Airlines has won the hearts of its customers by being completely empathic about the trials and tribulations of air travel. Not only is it one of the few airlines that still allow passengers to check their bags for free (up to two!), but it also understands how boring the flight attendant's mandatory safety-information speech can be, especially for seasoned travelers. So what did this creative, authentic company do?

Like Wistia, it decided to communicate an empathic message: *we know you hate this, so we're doing our best to make it entertaining for you.* That's why Southwest encourages flight attendants to present an animated demonstration, adding their own personality and comedic timing to entertain flyers. In an interview published in the trade publication *Skift*, Jeff Hamlett, captain and director of Southwest's Air Operation Assurance, said, "As long as all of the safety and regulatory requirements are met, our flight attendants are encouraged to make onboard safety briefings engaging through the use of humor, song, or other individual twists."[2]

How does Southwest know its strategy is working? Southwest customers post videos showcasing the flight attendants' safety demonstrations—everything from a stand-up comedy routine to a rap and even a farcical exotic dance. Several of those videos went viral, with one reaching more than twenty-four million views! *That's* how engaging a brand can be when it brings empathy to its experiences.

Alignment with the Media Channel

Besides getting the voice right and communicating empathy for your audience, delivering an authentic brand experience means aligning it with the media channel where people find it. Don't make the mistake of publishing the same content on all channels. Remember Marshall McLuhan: the medium is the message. That is, an authentic brand experience on Twitter will not automatically feel authentic on LinkedIn, even though both are social media platforms. Consumers spend time on each one for very different reasons, and when you keep the brand experience authentic to the nature of the channel you can much more easily break through.

Wendy's, the international fast-food chain, is a brand that gets it. Check out the super-conversational voice it uses to answer a question posted by a member of its Twitter audience (see figure 7-4).

As a fast-paced, real-time channel, Twitter is where people meet to converse about all kinds of things. Wendy's has found that by joining in these conversations in a snarky and fun way, it keeps its brand relevant to that audience. Compare Wendy's average engagement rate per post of around

FIGURE 7-4

six thousand likes, comments, and shares with that of McDonald's, which has a million more followers on Twitter but an average of comments, likes, and shares closer to only six hundred. That's because most of Mickey D's posts are product-focused and look like ads—not at all consistent with the channel and why people are on it. Wendy's engages in natural conversation that is aligned with the channel, and that makes all the difference.

That idea of authentically matching your message to the goal of the channel works for all brands, in any vertical. For example, Instagram is often thought of as a consumer channel, not conducive for business brands, but any brand that can match the authentic nature of the medium can break through on it. Notice the way WeWork matches its post to the spirit of Instagram in figure 7-5.

FIGURE 7-5

Source: WeWork Instagram feed.

It's clear from this post and its audience response that WeWork, like Wendy's, took the time to assess the unique nature of the particular media channel, which made its posts authentic to that moment. This isn't hard to do, because each channel makes it clear what's unique about it. Twitter limits your word count, making short, quippy conversations the ticket, while Instagram is unique in that the images are the focus of the engagement, not text. So aligning to Instagram just means shifting communication from text to images. Rather than trying to tell people via text that the WeWork offices are beautiful, well-designed, and great places to work, the company shows those things—using a natural voice, dialogue, and empathy. This is how WeWork aligned its brand experience authentically to break through.

The three qualities of the authentic element that we've just covered—voice, empathy, and alignment with the media channel—apply to every brand experience you create. Ignoring any of those qualities puts your brand in peril, just as paying attention to them can utterly transform how your audience perceives your brand.

Next we'll explore the final element in the context framework, which deeply relates to authenticity. It crowns the contextual effort by helping brands meet their audience in a space of shared purpose.

8.

Purposeful

Creating a Deeper Connection to the Brand beyond the Product

Creating contextual experiences at the highest level depends on getting clear on your brand's reason for being. Purposeful, the fifth and final element in the context framework, helps you achieve that clarity by shifting the focus of your brand experience beyond the product or service itself to a larger connection with your customer. Where authenticity is how well you are able to deliver against an expectation, purpose is the storyline behind the execution, the guiding force, the overarching theme. It is the heart of marketing.

Once you've articulated your brand's higher purpose, it becomes much easier to find natural ways to share that purpose with audiences at any moment, within any experience. What's more, you'll be able to build experiences that far exceed the limitations of what you sell. That's important, because there are only so many moments where your product belongs in a person's day, week, or month. You'll have to operate on a higher ground if you hope to become a greater part of your customers' lives.

Of course, those reasons for centering your brand around a higher purpose aren't radically new. Brands have been aligning with purposeful efforts for decades. Patagonia was one of the first to do so on a large scale, beginning in the 1970s. So while most marketers would agree that identifying with a purpose is a powerful differentiator, why don't more companies do it? Because it isn't easy to identify a purpose, much less to reach agreement on how to articulate it—and that leaves many brands struggling.

In 2017, Salesforce researched this very topic and found three main reasons brands had not begun any purposeful efforts:[1]

1. We don't want to risk putting out a message that polarizes our audience.

2. We are unsure how to connect our purpose to our marketing strategy.

3. We have insufficient executive buy-in on the articulation of our purpose.

I believe the reason behind the first issue is that businesses and their marketing teams mistake purpose for "social purpose." If the number-one reason is fear of polarizing their audience, then it makes sense that brands are looking mainly at social issues, which can be controversial.

But a brand's purpose can best be found within its own environment. All it takes is enlarging the view of what your brand's larger function in the world is and committing to your role in supporting it. Such commitment is key—purpose can't be faked or merely given lip service. But here's the best part: even putting marketing aside for a moment, when your company identifies and commits to a higher purpose, this action has an enormously positive effect on your people and your internal culture. As most everyone knows, branding starts internally.

Consider today's companies that have clearly articulated their purpose in alignment with their brand:

- Tesla, the electric car manufacturer: "To accelerate the world's transition to sustainable energy"

- Always, the feminine products manufacturer: "To give women confidence"

- Salesforce, software vendor: "To be a platform for change and improve the state of the world by serving the interests of all our stakeholders—employees, customers, partners, communities, and the environment"

Each of those companies elevated its thinking beyond the product or service itself to *a shared connection with its market*—the "market" being all stakeholders including partners, the community, and customers. Tesla isn't trying to make the best car; rather, it seeks a higher plateau of sustainability. Always isn't focused on feminine hygiene—it's focused on women's deeper emotions. The focus of those brands extends the company and its role beyond just being a producer to becoming a valued community member. That allows them more access to their market and deeper connections with their customers, creating a stronger brand. Being clear on your purpose is relatively simple; living it is the tricky part. How your brand executes against your purpose is the key to reaching a higher level of context in all of your brand engagements, from mass campaigns to highly personal, human-to-human interactions.

Like most of the other elements of context, purposeful lies on a continuum from less to more contextual.

The Purposeful Continuum

All levels of the continuum presented in the web graphic are equally purposeful and good, but not all achieve the same results (see figure 8-1). Brands must realize the differences in various types of purpose, their limitations, and effects.

At the lowest point of the purposeful line sits *corporate social responsibility (CSR)*. Brands like TOMS footwear and Patagonia use CSR as a brand-defining quality that generally works as a backdrop to all of their efforts. At the more contextual end, brands like Sambazon, a natural food and beverage company, invite their audiences to *cocreate* a brand experience—all in the name of a specific purpose shared between the company and customers.

FIGURE 8-1

The context framework (purposeful)

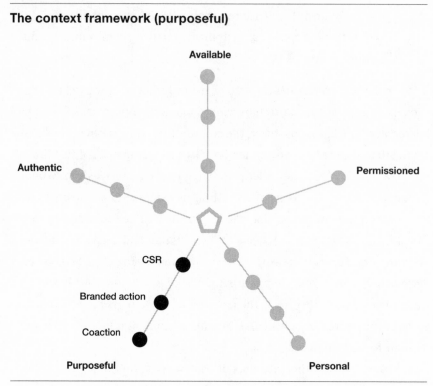

Corporate Social Responsibility

CSR is a body of communication that showcases a company's or brand's social consciousness. The CSR movement traces its roots back to 1953, with Howard R. Bowen's book *Social Responsibilities of the Businessman*, which defined CSR as follows: ". . . the obligation of businesses to pursue those policies, to make those decisions, or to follow those lines of action which are desirable in terms of the objectives and values of society."[2] Bowen and his many followers in the decades thereafter provided the theoretical grounds for companies to act more in line with the values of society, beyond just the value of profit.

Today brands express CSR in a variety of ways. They create reports to shareholders proving the company's commitment to lowering its carbon footprint. They donate a percentage of their profits to charities, or they publish blogs about staff volunteer days with causes like Habitat for Humanity. CSR has become increasingly common over the past decade, to the point that it is something consumers expect from companies large and small.

Using altruistic acts as a way to break through the noise is a good start, but it's limited in the context it can create, for a few reasons. First, these efforts fit squarely within the dynamics of the limited era, in which messages ruled the day and flowed in one direction. If you wanted to impress your audience, all you had to say was "Hey, we are donating 10% of every purchase you make to save the [insert your cause]." But as discussed earlier in this book, simply telling your audience something isn't effective anymore. They're not listening. Even if we're now messaging about something other than our products, we're still broadcasting. Second, most CSR causes fall low on the context spectrum because they're only tangentially related to the product or service. So while CSR is obviously a good thing for organizations to engage in, it won't be contextual—or effective—unless marketers find ways to interact with the brand's target consumers on the issue.

Branded Actions

More purposeful than CSR are branded actions—efforts to share a core purpose related to the brand, but without focusing on the product itself. Always, which makes feminine hygiene products, provides an outstanding example. For a number of years, Always had articulated its purpose as "giving women confidence," even using the phrase in its advertising. When it decided to look for new ways to align its purpose with its audience, Always started by conducting market research. This research was not a simple survey asking questions about confidence but deeper academic research found in journals of psychology and other sources—all in an effort to better understand how women's confidence changes over time.

The research showed that women's self-confidence drops the most between the ages of sixteen and twenty-four.[3] It also showed that girls' self-esteem drops twice as much as boys' during puberty. The worst part was that the data showed that women never regain their prepubescent level of self-esteem. If giving women confidence was its purpose, then Always knew it had to address the issues affecting women during those crucial years of their lives. According to the research, the main issue affecting girls' self-esteem was society's gender stereotype of associating power and strength with men and boys only. Messages that boys should not do things "like a girl" reinforced the stereotype that being like a girl made them powerless. The associated message, of course, was that girls weren't powerful or strong.

Company leaders at Always realized that to fulfill its purpose of giving women confidence, Always would need to take action to bust the stereotype and change what "like a girl" means. It decided to conduct an experiment in which young girls (prepubescent) and grown women in separate interviews were asked to do the same task. The resulting three-minute short film conveys a startling message, cutting back and forth between the girls and the grown women. When asked, for example, to "throw like a girl," the girls—who hadn't yet absorbed societal stereotypes—did a windup and delivered a pitch just like any professional ballplayer would. But the grown women made an awkward motion as if they'd never thrown a ball before. Similarly, when asked to "run like a girl," the young girls sprinted like Florence Griffith Joyner. But the grown women had absorbed all too well what was being asked by the instruction to "run like a girl"—they flailed their legs helplessly, acting out the stereotype. The stark contrast between the girls' perception and the grown women's perception of what it means to be "like a girl" broke through to huge audiences, which not only created profit for Always but also contributed to an important conversation about this issue.

The video was watched more than ninety *million* times, and the effort generated more than 177,000 #LikeAGirl tweets in the first three months. Among Always's target market, intent-to-purchase grew more than 50 percent. Most impressive was a study conducted after the video's release showing that almost 70 percent of women and 60 percent of men said "the video changed my perception of the phrase 'like a girl.'"

Even though this purpose-driven video was a mass campaign, the enormous number of shares under the hashtag #LikeAGirl proves that many people encountered Always through a contextual experience on social networks, and the force that produced that context marketing was clearly the brand's purpose and not its product. Remember that Always is a feminine hygiene product, so the fact that 60 percent of men claimed that the video changed their perception offers more evidence that this campaign worked largely through context, when women showed it to the men in their lives: the fathers of their daughters, their sons, uncles, and grandfathers.

Coaction

It's important to note that marketing is moving away from large, expensive campaigns like the Always video. Such mass, one-to-many campaigns will continue, but they will need to be connected to related contextual brand experiences. The good news is that there are many other tactics for sharing your purpose with your audience, where you aren't merely projecting messages but working with consumers in their own context. Perhaps the most effective way is through coaction.

Sambazon, which makes Acai berry–based food and beverages such as smoothies offers an award-winning[4] example of how a brand can focus on a shared purpose and cocreate actions with individuals without directly marketing its product. In May 2018, Sambazon asked its audience to help save thirty endangered species in thirty days by taking an individual action: people were asked to dye their hair purple and share a photo of their purple locks on social media with the tag #purplefortheplanet. For each person who did it, Sambazon would buy five acres of rainforest. Research into conservation science reveals that species go extinct largely because of habitat loss, and the majority of species diversification occurs in rainforests. Thus every 538 acres of rainforest preserved would actually save another species. For every one hundred people who participated, the effort could save one species, which, doing the math, means three thousand people would need to make the pledge in order to save thirty species. Plus, Acai berries grow in the rainforest, so Sambazon's purpose grew naturally out of its brand while also fulfilling a social purpose (a lesson in how your purpose can do both).

The program was a partnership between Sambazon and the Rainforest Trust's Save-an-Acre Program, which handled the actual purchase and protection of the forest. In addition to the marketing campaign, celebrity influencers like Olympic gold-medal gymnast Jordy Wieber (2012, United States) helped spread the word. The campaign was a huge success, with more than five thousand people taking part on Instagram alone. In the end, Sambazon, the Rainforest Trust, and thousands of individual people ended up saving more than thirty species of life from going extinct on our planet.

So how does saving endangered species help Sambazon? In several ways. First, it was able to work with its audience to accomplish a shared goal. Both the brand and plenty of consumers want to do good things for the planet, and here was one they could do together, strengthening the bond between the brand and its audience. Second, Sambazon leveraged its audience—meaningfully—to reach others *outside its network* in a highly contextual way.

How did it do it? The more than five thousand posts on Instagram, all mentioning Sambazon, weren't just posts; they were pictures of people with *purple hair*—a fairly drastic action to take—shared with thousands of their personal connections. This is social media gold, as dyeing your hair purple is sure to spur a comment or retweet from family and friends, who are more likely than a random viewer to share similar values. When those newly exposed to Sambazon through #purplefortheplanet next encountered the brand—in a store or when shopping online—they would have a positive image and a deeper connection to the brand already built in. This phenomenon is known as "digital word of mouth," and it is highly contextual. This is also the kind of result traditional mass campaigns spend a small fortune on to achieve. But Sambazon shows us how it's done in the infinite era: by working directly with individuals to accomplish a purposeful goal (focused on a healthier planet, not Sambazon's own product), and by exposing its brand to a highly targeted group of likely customers in a very contextual way.

Cotopaxi, the adventure clothing brand, also cocreates actions with individuals based on a shared purpose. The company was cofounded by Stephan Jacob, who wanted to merge his love of travel (particularly in South America—the brand is named after Cotopaxi, an Ecuadorean national park) with a poverty-fighting business model. Each customer's purchase would help provide a better life to people living in one of the world's poorest regions. But Jacob went beyond the social purpose of his company to fulfill the purpose of his apparel, which he says "represents the spirit of adventure, optimism, and determination" that he'd experienced during his time in Ecuador. Instead of simply broadcasting that message, Jacob brought that spirit to the cities where Cotopaxi customers and fans live by creating Questival events.

For example, people participating in the Questival 24 Adventure Races complete tasks in different categories, such as fitness, camping, service, and teamwork. One might craft a canoe out of cardboard and float a teammate in it for five seconds, while another person might donate a box of gently used clothing—or donate blood while wearing Dracula teeth. Each task has points associated with it, and at the end, points are tallied and the winners receive prizes. Questival events have become so beloved by Cotopaxi customers and fans that the list of participating cities in 2018 grew to more than fifty in the United States and Canada. People pay to attend, and they all share their adventures on social media using hashtags that expose others to Cotopaxi in a highly contextual way.

That same idea of cocreating actions that fulfill a deeper shared purpose works in all types of businesses, not just consumer goods and retail. At Salesforce, our purpose is to be a "platform for change," which means not only helping businesses succeed but also being a catalyst for improving the lives of others. To that end, its pioneering 1-1-1 corporate philanthropy model dedicates 1 percent of time, 1 percent of product, and 1 percent of our equity to help nonprofits achieve their missions. As a result, Salesforce employees have logged nearly five million volunteer hours throughout the world, contributed technology to power more than forty-five thousand nonprofit and higher education institutions, and provided more than $300 million in grants.

Salesforce has also translated that purpose to promote professional career growth worldwide through its Trailhead program, the education platform described earlier in this book. The results have been outstanding—for both Salesforce and our users. Trailhead has naturally drawn together its own community of professionals who are intensely focused on career growth and better business outcomes. To date, that Trailhead community has more than 1.8 million learners. Together they've completed more than fifteen million badges (certificates of completion for a course), sparking comments like this one from Gaurav Kheterpal, vice president of mobility and tech evangelism at Metacube: "I have a strong career, but more than that, I have become a member of a global tribe. This sense of belonging is something I never would have expected from a technology company."[5]

Digging into the data, Salesforce's customers who have joined Trailhead to improve their skills are more likely to advance their careers. In fact, one-fourth of those using Trailhead found a new job. This engagement with the brand on their shared purpose of crafting more meaningful and successful careers creates a deep loyalty in the audience and stronger bottom lines for both Salesforce and its customers. And the company did that not simply by broadcasting that it "supports career growth" but also by taking specific actions *with* its audience, using the highest levels of context to create exceptional outcomes.

Now that you understand purposeful, our tour of the elements of the context framework is complete. It is up to you to put it into practice. To do so, I suggest keeping the image of the framework on your table, desk, or conference room wall and look at it as you begin to craft your plans. Take each idea and map it on the framework, then ask yourself, can I do better? To create a better experience, simply move farther out along any one of the five elements. But the framework is also a diagnostic tool. Didn't receive the results you wanted? Plot the experience, and you'll see where it can be improved. This is how the framework functions as your guide to greater context in any moment.

Another powerful benefit of the framework is its ability to train your thinking when it comes to experiences. You'll begin to see experiences as connected moments rather than single events. For example, if the brand experience you created was lacking permission, you'll now begin to look at preceding moments to see where you can gain that permission, ensuring greater success in the future.

With the framework covered, you should have a solid idea of what makes a contextual experience and how they compound and multiply. But those are only the beginning steps of what it takes to transition to the context marketing model. Next we need to look at how we connect these experiences across an ever-expanding customer journey and leverage them to create motivation—driving the demand we seek.

In part three, we'll dig into the tactical details of executing the context marketing model—and transform your company into a contextual organization, starting with a look at how to transition your idea of marketing from campaigns to ever-flowing journeys, and all that it entails.

HOW TO MARKET BRANDS IN THE INFINITE MEDIA ERA

9.

Shifting from Campaigns to Customer Journeys

We've seen how the infinite media era has fundamentally expanded the way we define "brand experience." But the new era has also transformed how marketing gets *done*. In this final part of the book, we'll examine strategies for executing context marketing.

Think about how marketing campaigns once worked. They were like tidal waves, drenching as many people as possible with a brand's message and call to action. That mass of people filled the top of the sales funnel and—fingers crossed—a good number would convert to a sale and fall out the bottom as a customer.

As context marketers, we are trading in the funnel to become something much smarter than a simple catching device: we are guides, moving every customer through a personal journey. The new goal is to help each individual take the next step along the path, followed by the next one, and so on. As we'll see, in some ways the new customer journey functions like a free-running river. It's an ongoing system of organized brand experiences that constantly flows, with numerous individual currents that converge and diverge in a multitude of ways.

Context is how we guide the consumer along, providing the motivation to continue forward, wherever the person happens to be on the journey. To connect or reconnect an individual to the journey, we leverage *triggers*, which occur along the entire customer journey, not just at the beginning—because not all buyers start at the beginning (again, we are not filling a funnel). In context marketing, we rely on two kinds of triggers: natural and targeted. As you'll recall from part one, natural triggers are those that individuals come across on their own, in the course of their day: your sick dog, an email from a friend, or even seeing a new gray hair in the mirror. Targeted triggers are those that your brand proactively deploys: sending an email about a new offering, engaging with consumers on social media, or maybe setting up a chatbot on the brand website. Marketers can use both kinds of triggers to motivate consumers in a contextual way, as we'll explore in depth in the next chapter.

Note that the number of triggers along a journey, and the range of brand experiences you'll need to maintain as a result, can grow exponentially, depending on the size of your market and the complexity of the sale. That's why the only way to really scale context marketing is by leveraging *automated programs*, which we'll examine closely later in this part. For now, understand that such programs are the key to scaling personal context. The programs do this by leveraging a wide range of data, combined with a new layer of technology to create bespoke experiences at scale. In other words, automated programs—such as lead nurturing, onboarding, and chatbots—are the always-on current that links the individual experiences and keeps your prospects floating downstream toward purchase, and beyond. When a prospect starts "heading to shore," so to speak, automations alert your human staff to come to that consumer's aid and provide the needed nudge.

Part three also examines a new method—*agile*—that marketers today will need in order to manage and optimize the seemingly endless networks of brand experiences and customer journeys under their care. Finally, we'll see where the infinite media era has already started heading, toward a new business model: the context marketing model, which includes new leadership and tools for marketing departments to measure and show the value of what they do.

But first, this chapter examines what's needed to begin the crucial work of mapping customer journeys and carrying out the intricate execution required: customer interviews to help you learn exactly what individuals are doing at each stage in the journey.

All Journeys Need a Map

Shifting from campaigns to constantly flowing and converging journeys is an evolution that few brands have made successfully (remember that only 16 percent of brands are high performers). Many have at least moved away from large, single-message campaigns in favor of smaller, more targeted messages that are pushed out more frequently, but most of these efforts are still focused on conversion and don't rely on context to reach audiences.

Like any good marketing strategy, context marketing begins with in-depth customer research. This is a step that cannot be skipped or approximated. To understand the context in which customers move through their journeys, you'll need to conduct personal interviews with current customers and groups of people you want as customers. These are not your typical interviews or focus groups, and a survey will not suffice. Contextual marketing requires a deeper level of inquiry, focused on the customer's journey and the specifics of his or her natural movement along it. From those interviews you will create "buyer personas," or representatives of specific groups of people who act in similar ways. This will allow for a more personal approach.

To learn more about this type of customer research, I spoke with Ardath Albee, a leading thinker in persona development and journey mapping and the author of *Digital Relevance and eMarketing Strategies for the Complex Sale*. Her best advice? Remember that "these are interviews, not interrogations." In other words, your skill in making your interviewees comfortable is almost more important than the questions you ask. Allow them to lead the conversation. If they go off on a tangent that's still related to things you need to learn, let them do so. Some of your best insights will come from simply listening and getting answers to questions you never thought to ask.

What's more, when asking your interview questions, never refer to your product by name, Albee says. Instead, talk about the product or service category. People will then speak freely, without fear that they're criticizing your brand. You'll also learn what they find most valuable about the products or services they use.

As with everything else in the infinite media era, what you need to learn from your market research has dramatically changed. Effective customer journeys don't uncover just key characteristics like age, geography, and demographics; that's targeting data that can be obtained through simple observation. Rather, your context marketing research interviews will aim to uncover three key pieces of information: what your audience members are *doing, thinking, and feeling* at each stage of the customer journey.[1]

Specifically, your interview questions about what consumers are *doing* will reveal what actions people are taking at each stage, such as searching the web, using social media, asking friends, or visiting a retail store. Your questions about what they are *thinking* really dig into what your customers want to achieve in each stage. And your questions about what consumers are *feeling* help you uncover people's emotions related to each stage, such as anxiety or excitement.

What follows here are sample questions I've structured for your consumer interviews. You'll see there is one set of questions for each of the six stages of the new customer journey, which I introduced in chapter 2: *ideation, awareness, consideration, purchase, customer,* and *advocacy.* Note that the kinds of personal consumer interviews outlined here require a great deal of work, time, and resources. Be sure you prepare for them and have the support you'll need from various levels in the organization. Note, too, that each set of questions ends with the same blanket query: *What did you do next?* The answers you receive will help you understand the consumer's viewpoint about the journey's progress.

Ideation Stage

The first set of questions is designed to discover the circumstances under which the customer's journey began.

- **Doing:** What publications do you read? What social channels do you use, and whom do you follow on various platforms? (This will also give you insight into shared passions to guide your purposeful brand experiences, as discussed in chapter 8.)

- **Thinking**: What was the initial thing that got you interested in this type of product (or service)?

- **Feeling**: Have you bought anything in this category before? How prepared did you feel in your search? What emotion best describes your feelings at this stage?

What did you do next?

Awareness Stage

Here you uncover *how the customer transitioned from an initial idea* to a solution, and why he or she chose this option. Remember, the riskier the purchase, the more questions people will ask, so it's important you know which questions they ask, in what order, and the length of time they spent in this stage.

- **Doing**: What questions did you ask? Where did you look for answers? Were you able to find what you were looking for?

- **Thinking**: What were you expecting when you started to look for solutions? What did you learn from those questions and answers? What questions were never answered sufficiently?

- **Feeling**: How would you describe your experience of the process?

What did you do next?

Consideration Stage

Here, your questions should pinpoint your audience's decision-making process for determining which companies made the short list and which ones were eventually crossed off and why. Again, it is imperative you know the number of questions, the order, and how long it took them to find satisfying answers.

- **Doing**: How did your search terms change as you zeroed in on the best options?

- **Thinking:** What concerns did you have going into the decision-making process? What options did you consider for fulfilling your need / solving your problem?

- **Feeling:** How did the process make you feel? Was it easy to find the information you were seeking? Were you satisfied with the amount of information you had to make your decision? What was the best experience you remember from this stage of your journey?

What did you do next?

Purchase Stage

The purchase stage has many moving parts, and the sooner your marketing team optimizes for them, the better. Be sure to listen for the particular situations each person faced, how their concerns were addressed—which experience addressed them best—and how those things affected their purchase.

- **Doing:** How did you make your purchase? Was a salesperson involved? If so, did he or she help or detract from the experience?

- **Thinking:** What led you to make the purchasing decision? What did you want to happen that didn't happen during the purchase? Was the purchasing process easy?

- **Feeling:** Were you confident in your purchase? What questions remained unanswered, if any? How did the purchase process make you feel?

What did you do next?

Customer Stage

The customer stage is specific to how the individual uses your product or service and the customer experience. Each customer will have a different reason, or goal, for using your brand. The better you can guide customers through the steps of achieving their goal, the better their experience and the longer they will stay customers. These are interviews you need to conduct *with your actual customers*, and many of these answers can be expanded on from actual usage data, if it is available.

- **Doing**: How often do you engage with the tool, product, or service? Which aspects do you engage with most?

- **Thinking**: What do you hope to accomplish with this product or service?

- **Feeling**: Are you confident in your ability to use the tool, service, product? How does using it make you feel? Have you been frustrated with the experience? Do you feel it is meeting your needs?

What will you do next?

Advocacy Stage

If you have advocates, ask them why they love your product. If you do not have advocates, find advocates of other brands and ask them what makes them love that company, service, or product to the point they will advocate for it.

- **Doing**: When you truly love a brand, how do you share your opinions? Do you ever post about brands on social media? Have you ever participated in a formal brand community or group event?

- **Thinking**: What compels you to become an advocate?

- **Feeling**: How do your favorite brands make you feel? What brand experiences won you over?

What will you do next as an advocate for [the brand they mentioned]?

By focusing on the three areas of doing, thinking, and feeling as a guide for your basic questions in each stage of the customer journey, you'll be able to uncover the larger questions that your brand must address for each "buyer persona" that you identify, as we'll see in the next section.

Buyer Personas and the Customer Journey

Say you're a computer storage device manufacturer. The questions asked in the personal interviews just described will uncover some particular categories of people who make up your consumers. These answers will form the basis of the buyer personas for whom you'll be building customer journeys. You may discover more personas than you worked with in the past, or you may find more than one journey within each persona. In the case of our hypothetical storage device manufacturer, you may have dozens of buyer personas—college students, artists and designers, small-business owners, corporate IT heads, hospital administrators, and more. Despite there being many possibilities, I'd suggest you start by focusing on only one or two. Choose those personas that represent the largest population of your customers.

Now you'll give each buyer persona a person's name and face. You can use the names and faces of actual customers, or you can make them up. Beyond a name and face, you should also include demographics (age, location, gender) and psychographics (feelings, goals, behaviors) to develop each persona. The answers you received during your customer interviews regarding what individuals were *doing, thinking, and feeling* at various stages of the customer journey will guide you.

For example, from your interviews you'll discover what each persona's "top goals" are, both in general and according to particular stages of the journey. You'll know what their biggest daily problems or obstacles are and when those arise, as well as what particular triggers drive each persona to act. There will be a lot of other information that you ascertain from your interviews; that's the power of using such a simple set of questions that illuminate larger truths. But when writing up your buyer personas, try to stay focused on the high-level topics so that, ideally, each persona fits on a single page.

In the case of our hypothetical storage device manufacturer, one buyer persona the interviewers uncovered is someone they call "Designer Danielle," a corporate graphic designer (see figure 9-1). Note how much the brand was able to infer about this buyer persona from consumer interviews,

FIGURE 9-1

Buyer persona example

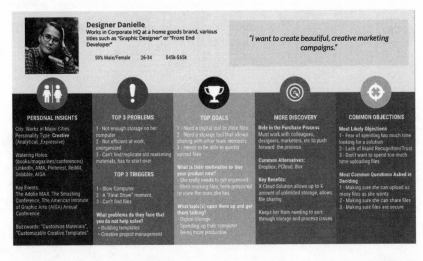

Source: Melissa Randall, "Using Customer Journey Maps and Buyer Personas Templates for Website Strategies," Lean Labs, April 18, 2019, https://www.lean-labs.com/blog/using-customer-journey-maps-and -buyer-personas-templates-for-website-strategies. Used with permission of Lean Labs.

including some of the topics just discussed in the previous paragraph, such as goals, problems, and triggers that drive action.

Next, it's time to map out the journey or journeys for each persona. You'll base these on the qualitative data you gathered about differing goals among the people you interviewed. This doesn't have to be complicated; think of it as a guide. Most important is identifying the major triggers for each persona across the journey and then capturing that "doing, thinking, and feeling" information along each stage. (We'll cover triggers in depth in the next chapter.)

Figure 9-2 offers an example of a customer journey map—Designer Danielle's. But understand that there are many ways to go about such mapping, and you can find a variety of templates online, each with slight differences. For example, the template in figure 9-2 refers to the customer journey stages as steps (1–4) rather than the six-stage journey I develop in this book that begins with *ideation* and ends with *advocacy*. My point is that it's OK to use your own language as you develop your buyer persona journey. This is your internal document, and it's best to use words your

FIGURE 9-2

Sample customer journey map

Customer Journey Map - Ideal			Persona: Designer Danielle	
			Problem: Not Enough Storage For Design Files	
STAGES	STEP #1	STEP #2	STEP #3	STEP #4
DOING	Customer knows she has a problem - not enough storage. She searches for ways to create more space on her computer, asks other designers and coworkers what they're doing. She tells her supervisor, but no action is taken.	Customer is doing research about her problem. She googles tactics to decrease file size, starts comparing external hard drives to cloud storage. She finds an article you wrote directly comparing the two. She clicks on the CTA for a free trial and a limited time offer for a $5 Amazon gift card.	Customer tries your solution to her problem. She uses the trial. Immediately, the brand sends her a few emails, with a video and guides on how to organize her files better and decrease the size.	Customer uses your solution. The platform uploads files quickly. There's no limit to her storage.
THINKING	Customer is thinking: Do I need to get external storage? How much does that cost? Will work pay for it?	Customer is thinking: I get the differences now. I can sign up for this trial and start storing stuff right away, plus, I can use that gift card later. Win win.	Customer is thinking: I can move all of my files over and delete the old ones from my laptop. I'm not getting charged yet, so this is free.	Customer is thinking: This is great. I don't need to worry about this anymore.
FEELING	Customer is feeling: Apprehensive (I don't want to spend x much), Clueless (I don't even know where to start.)	What is the customer feeling? Relieved (She finally understands the problem and feels like she has a decent solution)	What is the customer feeling? Excited. Her laptop is running faster and she finally feels organized.	What is the customer feeling? Relief. The problem is solved for her.
CUSTOMER EXPERIENCE	Customer is experiencing: Really slow computer, constant reminders that she's out of storage or running out of storage.	Customer is experiencing: Ease. She knows exactly what to do, was easy to make a choice.	What is the customer experiencing during this? Productivity. She's moving files over and getting all of the info she needs to organize them.	Customer is experiencing: Ease. She's getting everything she needs and more from the platform.
OPPORTUNITIES	What can you do to improve the customer experience? Create TOFU guides that explain how to Get more storage on your computer, quickly, Or how to decrease the size of your files	What can we do to improve the customer experience? Create chatbot for the website to answer some of Customer's easier questions, might be able to get her on the phone with a salesperson sooner.	What can we do to improve the customer experience? Keep in contact with Customer. She's having a good experience for now, but you want to retain her.	What can we do to improve the customer experience? Check up with Customer. Make sure she's getting the support she needs.

Source: Melissa Randall, "Using Customer Journey Maps and Buyer Personas Templates for Website Strategies," Lean Labs, April 18, 2019, https://www.lean-labs.com/blog/using-customer-journey-maps-and-buyer-personas-templates-for-website-strategies. Used with permission of Lean Labs.

company is already familiar with. There isn't a right or wrong. The most important aspects of the customer journey are that you *have* one that you can follow, that you break the journey down into defined stages, and that the journey is shared widely across your organization.

As we see in figure 9-2, Danielle begins her journey because she wants the ability to create richer digital experiences while keeping her current computer. That's the initial trigger that drives her to start searching online and talking to her friends and family about her desire (ideation stage). Her search brings up a wide range of options, creating new thoughts, emotions, and actions. She becomes apprehensive because she doesn't want to spend a lot of money on a solution, and she is clueless about where to begin. So she turns to Google and begins to batch questions, and she realizes that she has a few options, such as cloud storage or an external hard drive. Again, she discusses the options she's found with friends and colleagues and looks online to compare her options (awareness stage).

From there she's able to narrow her search down to a few brands she feels are credible (consideration stage), which leads to her next thoughts: just how do each of these solutions compare with one another? Since all the solutions are similar, she wants to try out the products. Continuing her investigation, she reads an article on one brand's site, and the brand (the storage device company) uses a chatbot to offer a thirty-day free trial. She likes that idea and accepts the offer. She is excited to receive the device in the mail and begins to use it. A day after the package arrives, she's happy to receive an email from a setup specialist at the company to follow up on any remaining questions and ensure she knows how best to use the product. As she familiarizes herself with the device, she's relieved to find her computer runs faster now that her files are stored externally. Thrilled at how easy it was and feeling supported in her decision, she keeps the product and becomes a customer (purchase and customer stages).

As I've said, it's important that customer journey maps be shared with the larger organization at all levels so that all members can align themselves with them. To further that alignment you can add your brand's response to each situation. Again, there is no right or wrong way to do this. The map in figure 9-2 includes a row titled "Customer Experience," which boils down each stage of the customer journey into a short sentence or two. The map also includes another row, "Opportunities," which provides a draft of the brand's high-level strategy to respond to the customer. These kinds of simple statements help align everyone around the persona's needs and how the brand plans to respond in each stage of the journey.

Danielle's journey takes place over several days, and as noted in her story, along the way the storage device brand leveraged a few triggers (such as the chatbot and the support email) to motivate her to continue and to guide her to the next steps.

That brings us to the next chapter: how to set up triggers. These will be the key moments connecting, or reconnecting, each individual to the journey. Your interviews will have pointed you to many of these key moments, and now we'll learn how brands can leverage the context framework to motivate action within those moments. That means meeting buyers early, keeping them moving, supporting them once they become customers, and leveraging brand advocates to keep the cycle of context turning.

10.

Triggers along the Journey

Meeting your brand's audience at opportune moments along their individual journeys depends on understanding how triggers work. You'll be using triggers to nudge consumers forward—employing both the *natural triggers* that occur within the context of their days and the *targeted triggers* that you as a marketer will create to motivate consumers in a contextual way.

In this chapter we'll look at how to engage triggers to meet buyers early and often along the journey, to keep consumers moving forward through each stage, to transition them to become better customers, and to leverage the power of your advocates, who keep the cycle of context flowing.

Let's begin with how to use triggers to jump into the customer journey as early as possible.

Meeting Buyers Early (and Often) along the Journey

One of the most common natural triggers in a consumer's life, and one that's good at starting individuals on their path in the ideation stage, is contact with trusted sources in a personal network. In the infinite era, social media makes it far easier for marketers to be a part of such moments; the tricky part is breaking through in close context so that people will find your brand experience authentic. To break through organically and trigger next steps, you need to leverage the cycle of context.

For example, "influencer marketing" is an easy way for a brand to become organically part of a consumer's life. Influencers are individuals who promote or recommend a brand or product to their social audience, and they can often kick off or reengage a journey. Where most brands are aware of influencer marketing, too often they apply it in traditional marketing style, pushing out a new product with a highly paid celebrity endorsement. This onetime hit works more like a campaign—"one and done"—*very* limited era.

To become contextual, influencer marketing is best accomplished as a continuous drip spread across a number of smaller audiences, even nano-audiences. Sapna Maheshwari, writing in the *New York Times*, sums up why nanoinfluencers (with followers as few as one thousand) are so effective: "Their lack of fame is one of the qualities that makes them approachable. When they recommend a shampoo or a lotion or a furniture brand on Instagram, their word seems as genuine as advice from a friend."[1]

The watchmaker Daniel Wellington used small-sized influencers to turn its startup into a $100 million business. One of its target personas was the millennial buyer, who is heavily influenced by experiences on Instagram. From interviews, DW marketers derived three key topics to cover: fashion, travel, and lifestyle. They knew that by meeting their audience in the context of influencers posting about these topics, people might get the idea that they would like a sleek, stylish watch. The watch was never the focus of the Instagram photo, so the influencers could stay true to their own focus on fashion or travel.

Daniel Wellington is a good example of a company that follows the context framework, delving deeply into being purposeful (element #5) by fostering coaction with customers. After influencers post images to their channels, the brand reposts some of the images on its own Instagram account, and with each post the cycle of context compounds for greater effect. Such a targeted trigger is just one example of how identifying the key moments from your interviews—and working to continually be part of them—can drive growth for your brand for many years. That's how, in 2017—six years after its launch—the watchmaker grew its audience by another 31 percent, year over year, resulting in four million active and engaged fans: an Instagram audience almost four times bigger than Tag Heuer's and Fossil's audiences *combined*.

Triggers also work well for entering the customer journey when a high-consideration, risky purchase is on the table, such as business software. HubSpot, for example, has mastered the use of natural and targeted triggers at the early stages of its customers' journeys. To make sure potential customers find the company, it publishes content to its blog so it appears in search results, answering people's questions in the moment. Very few of the articles talk about the company or its products. The majority focus on a wide range of other questions the company knows its audience is asking. Each piece of content answering a question and guiding them on to the next, triggering the journey to continue.

Those triggers do more than just bring people to the company blog; they drive demand. HubSpot found a very high correlation between blog readership and purchasing, which is why it put such a heavy focus on its blogs and content. The company uses its content to ensure HubSpot arises organically in those moments along the customers' journey, but it also works to take that experience further, with the use of targeted triggers. Before deploying a targeted execution, HubSpot first seeks permission by asking you to subscribe to the blog. It then uses that subscription to trigger a deeper connection to the brand. In the words of Anum Hussain, a former HubSpot growth marketer behind that effort, "Our goal isn't to shove content into inboxes; it is to provide something worth reading." If the company can get you to desire its content, or at least think it's great, then your odds of reading the blog increase, as do the odds of you then becoming a customer. The result for HubSpot? The blog is the source for one out of every five purchases of the company's product.[2]

To showcase that value, HubSpot uses a very specific technique to transition new subscribers, called "onboarding." I'll dive deeper into the onboarding tactic later in the chapter, but for now notice how HubSpot uses a simple series of emails as targeted triggers to not only reengage consumers in the HubSpot journey but also foster desire for the products and motivation to read future posts. Usually when a brand gets a new subscriber, the consumer is treated the same as current subscribers. The consumer is added to the list of subscribers, and the next blog post published is sent directly to his or her inbox.

But is your next blog post your best post? Odds are it isn't, not even close. So rather than starting off the relationship with subpar content, HubSpot jump-starts it by featuring its best. Each new subscriber is taken on a *personal* onboarding journey via email, where he or she is introduced to the top-three-performing blog posts first, only after which is the individual placed on the regular cadence to receive the newest blog content. Those onboarding emails have created twice as much engagement as other emails that HubSpot has sent. Such triggers bring the subscribers back to the site while increasing their desire and trust in the brand's content.

HubSpot has used this model to grow rapidly and consistently. Today it creates more than fifty good pieces of content per week to publish across various channels, ensuring HubSpot is *there for consumers in those important moments* during that initial ideation stage of the journey.[3] By being early in the journey and building strong trust, the company helps shape the ideas and journeys of its subscribers. As Hussain said, HubSpot isn't focused on just creating content but rather creating value, and it does. This method is so effective at driving downstream purchases that the company has given up exhibiting at trade shows to reallocate more resources to support it.[4]

How to Keep the Customer Moving Forward

Once you've met your potential customers in the ideation stage, you can use triggers to keep them moving ahead through the next four stages of the journey: awareness, consideration, purchase, and customer. Let's look at each in turn.

Motivating Buyers in the Awareness Stage

Awareness kicks off a more active stage, distinguished by questions your buyers use to better refine their needs and determine solutions or methods for reaching their goals. Thus your need to account for the sequence of questions (batches) asked (which you should have assembled from your interviews)—*in the channel where they are asking them.* Answering those questions is how we trigger next steps. That's not a new idea, yet brands often fall short in accounting for the number and batches in their buyers' journeys. The more questions you're prepared to answer with your content and human-to-human contact, the greater trust your brand will build and better positioned it will be as the preferred solution.

Your interviews about the awareness stage reveal a wide range of questions, far past your product or category keywords. For example, when Pardot (now a Salesforce company) was first selling marketing automation, it was a new category of technology; so many people who needed it weren't even aware of the term for it. In fact, progressive consumers who began their journey searching for "marketing automation" were probably already in the consideration stage, having become aware of the solution. At the time, email tools were the closest thing to marketing automation, and we knew from our interviews that our core audience was searching for "email best practices" not because they wanted to buy a new tool but because their goal was to be more effective marketers. To meet them in context, we answered their questions about new email marketing best practices, with one of the best practices being how email marketing can be automated and drive much higher results. You'll find this is still the case: 50 percent of the top answers for the search "email best practices" come from marketing automation vendors. *That's* a strong natural trigger.

Other triggers found during these batches include social question-and-answer sites, such as Reddit and Quora. You can learn about opportunities there and on other social media sites by engaging in social listening, a powerful way to meet individuals when they are talking about you or related topics. The Salesforce 2016 *State of Marketing* report found high-performing marketing organizations to be 8.8 times more likely to use social listening programs than underperformers.[5] They know where to listen, what to listen for, and how to respond.

Answers to your interview/consumer research questions about what the buyer is "doing" (see chapter 9) will point you to the channels where people are asking questions or engaging in conversations that you should be joining. Social listening happens in a few ways, many of them automated (more on this in the next chapter). Some social channels have "walled gardens," meaning you need to join a relevant community and use notification tools to "listen." LinkedIn is a key example for enterprise questions, as Nextdoor is for local purchases. You must be listening on those channels and respond when notified of a conversation.

Open social networks, such as Facebook, Twitter, and Instagram, allow for large-scale searches, so you can listen for any keywords across the entire network and apply a wide range of filters, such as geography or #hashtag, to make sure you listen to a more targeted audience.

When you answer a question in any channel, *do not refer directly to your product*. And it is always better if the response comes from an individual, one of your staff or a brand advocate, human-to-human. Answers from your brand's account will seem inherently biased and won't be trusted as much. You can set up alerts when your people need to respond (again, more about this in the next chapter). The program(s) can listen, identifying those moments so you can target a reply to the individual driving him or her forward. Again, a combination of consistency by constantly listening to the natural triggers and responding in context wins the day.

Note that when your staff or advocates respond to questions, they should focus only on the immediate question and the next step in the buyer's journey, not the sale. This is how motivation is fostered—not by trying to sell but rather by harnessing the existing action to guide the consumer forward. That's how you create value for the consumer, breaking through and building trust. The less people know about the product or solution they need, the more anxiety they'll have at this stage, and the less trust they will have in the answers they encounter. Creating articles with titles like "5 Things to Know" that aim to clarify issues surrounding your product or service can go a long way toward easing the kind of anxiety consumers experience during this stage. Here, too, the writer may mention your brand or be affiliated with it, but not promote it directly. If you answer questions fully and often, in a number of channels used by your buyer personas, you will build awareness of your brand in a contextual way.

Creating Triggers in the Consideration Stage

In the consideration stage, individuals in your audience become prospects who are developing a shortlist of vendors. They are going to purchase; the question now is finding the best fit for their needs. Based on your consumer interviews, you'll see that you have a whole new batch of questions to answer. Again, you must meet your prospects where they're looking—and enlist the sales department only when prospects request a conversation.

Questions buyers ask at this stage are focused on products and customer experience, and your answers must be detailed enough to satisfy discerning buyers. Whether your product is high-consideration or low-consideration, there are two triggers that I recommend you employ as soon as possible: (1) reviews and (2) product or service trials. People want to hear from others who have experienced your product or service, or better yet, they want to try it for themselves.

To get reviews, you must ask for them. The main problem is that everyone is asking, and reviews require quite a commitment from your customers: they have to navigate the review channel, such as Yelp or TripAdvisor, which often requires that they set up a profile, then they must write their review. Knowing this, you must offer ways to make it easier for them—and it never hurts to add an incentive, such as a 20 percent off promo code or free glass of champagne on their next visit to your establishment.

Backcountry, the outdoor outfitter, could use its Gearhead program (described in an earlier chapter) to personally reach out to customers about posting reviews. It could provide customers with a link that takes them to the exact page on the website where they want the review posted.

A human-to-human conversation, or note, before the customer writes the review is worth the investment here, because someone within your organization can inform the customer about issues related to the product being reviewed. If people are concerned about a product shrinking after washing, for example, your staff member could direct the reviewer to address that. They can also encourage customers to simply tell their story using as many details as possible. When you are triggering your customers to write a review, such information will help guide them, as will including in your email examples of great reviews.

Once the customer has left a review, someone should reach back out and say thank you. This should be done in a very personal way, but not online or as a response to their review. A study by Cornell University in 2016 found that when brands engaged with the majority of their positive reviews on a review site (even with simple responses like "glad you had a good time"), they actually created a negative effect on total revenue.[6]

Product trials are another significant trigger you can use in the consideration stage. If your service is online and lends itself to a trial program, you should be allowing such trials if you don't already. But even consumer goods can be given a try with the help of technology. Retail brands including Asics have adopted True Fit, a software allowing people to type in what size they wear in their favorite brands and then True Fit matches the fit or size of the online product based on that data. For example, if your favorite shoes are New Balance 910 in size 9.5, True Fit can tell you exactly what shoe size to buy in another brand to get the same fit. Virtual reality is also making it possible for brands such as Sephora to release a VR makeup app to help its buyers make better purchasing decisions by seeing what they would look like wearing the makeup or lip color in real time.

Each of these tools also has the ability to provide data, and thus become a platform for additional targeted triggers. The Sephora app, for example, can keep track of the products used and instantly spawn offers for those products in-app, or pass off the data to use in other channels (for example, the website). So when consumers return to the app, they are offered those products they spent the most time with (assuming they didn't already purchase), along with an incentive. Sephora can also send a triggered experience via the app, such as offering a full makeover in-store with the products and including a call to action in the form of picking a date and time. This triggers customers to move to the next step in the journey: getting the product in their hands.

Triggers in the Purchase Stage

In the purchase stage, each buyer persona will buy differently after varying levels of consideration. Knowing *how* and *why* your personas buy is very important, and your interviews will point you in the right direction. In general there is still some anxiety at this stage, which can be assuaged by a salesperson—human or not—as long as they are completely knowledgeable. That's why it is an excellent idea to share with your company's sales leadership the questions you discover during your interviews: your sales associates must be empowered to answer the common questions instantly, with easy access to any information they don't know off the top of their heads.

In 2018, a report looking at 6,000 consumers and their retail habits found that 73 percent of consumers had visited a retail store within the past week,[7] noting that knowledgeable sales associates were among the most helpful factors in the consumers making their final purchase decision. Brands such as Design Within Reach (DWR) provide sales associates with iPads equipped with software that allows them to answer any question consumers pose—about materials, options, availability, and even delivery date. Very soon I expect this information will be made accessible to customers online, so they can ask Alexa, "Where can I find a Mies van de Rohe chair within 50 miles?" This will give a heavy advantage to those brands that can answer these questions by making their inventory easily accessible and searchable in real time.

Where natural triggers ensure you are found, targeted triggers can bring your potential buyers back and get them to take action. Lego created a targeted trigger on Facebook, with the goal to reengage website visitors who had not bought a product. The trigger was a highly automated effort deployed only to those web visitors who hadn't been back to the website in thirty days, and who hadn't purchased anything in the past fourteen. The trigger was deployed via an ad on Facebook, enticing the individual to engage with Ralph the Lego Giftbot.

As I mentioned earlier in the book, ads do have a place and time, and this is a great example. The ad wasn't used to place product back in people's faces; rather, it was used to help them accomplish their goal: finding the perfect gift. The bot was a conversational interface and through dialogue the bot understood their needs, suggested products, and even ordered those products for them—all in Facebook Messenger. The trigger drove 25 percent of all online sales in 2017. But remember, we're talking here about just the tail end of a journey when a brand helped consumers accomplish the final task.

Another significant part of the purchase stage is configuring the purchase and determining final details like delivery. Recall the IKEA example from earlier in the book. Its addition of TaskRabbit allowed Ikea to assist with consumer goals for easy delivery and assembly in the same moment as the purchase. The final bit of motivation to get someone to purchase usually requires a targeted trigger (such as the TaskRabbit option) to help ease the transition. The desire is there, but we can remove any obstacles to the final step taking place. Identifying those obstacles comes from your consumer interviews (see chapter 9), leaving it up to you to solve them.

For complex purchases where you need to involve the sales department, you can pinpoint the specific obstacle by the standard process of objection identification. For example, a good salesperson will simply ask, "What is keeping you from moving forward?" Once the salesperson knows those answers, he or she can work to solve for them. If you have a sales team in place, those obstacles are already being identified and overcome. However, you should ensure you're aware of them too so you can begin to lay the groundwork earlier in the journey. By addressing obstacles to purchase earlier on, you can use your content to teach consumers an alternative option, or better yet, take them down a different path where the obstacle doesn't exist; or even better, when they reach the end the obstacle has been flipped and becomes a feature. For example, a product competing in a marketplace where it may lack more advanced features, often requiring extensive set up, could use early stage content to set the buyers requirements and make "ease of use" a key feature they should look for in a solution.

Using Targeted Triggers to Transition Buyers into Customers

Once you have a new buyer, triggers can help your brand create better experiences for the individual in many ways, thus increasing purchases and extending the lifetime value of that purchaser. As buyers transition to becoming customers, you will have a new goal: helping them get the full value of your product, tool, or service. Your interviews will have pointed you to the specific goals of your buyer personas. For example, the customer may be seeking self-esteem, better business outcomes, or better ways to perform a task. You can craft triggers to help customers accomplish almost any chosen goal(s).

Recall that HubSpot used the powerful trigger technique of onboarding to transition readers into subscribers by sending emails focused directly at the individual customer. So now we face another transition period: to move the buyer to becoming a customer, the onboarding trigger might come in the form of a chatbot greeting them on their next log-in, or perhaps a series of emails spanning their first tender weeks as a customer.

The goal of the onboarding at this point is to trigger individuals to take the steps that your best customers take, such as asking for help, getting it, and taking first steps. Essentially, you'll want to remove barriers between customers and the value they seek. Onboarding campaigns work because they drive revenue across the customer life cycle. In a discussion of onboarding with Nicholas Holmes, former industry manager at Google and current marketing director at Nickelled (onboarding specialist), he shared the following example, which mathematically shows how effective such triggers are at driving motivation and much higher profits.

Starting with the assumption that your business has 1,000 users, let's say that every year 5 percent of your existing customers churn, or quit using your service or product. In addition to your existing customers, there is a 50 percent new customer churn rate, meaning, of the customers who sign up today, only half will stay for more than a month. And for easy math, let's say you're adding 100 new users monthly. You are losing half of those 100 users every month because of problems with their onboarding, meaning they're not finding the value from your brand that they feel they should be. To recap: in terms of our total churn, 5 percent of it is happening among existing users ($1{,}000 \times .05 = 50$), and 50 percent is happening among new users ($100 \times .5 = 50$), so overall churn is 100 users per month, 10 percent of the total customer base. The number of users lost over one year (by month) would look something like figure 10-1.

Holmes points out if you do the math in this scenario, you will find that the business is stagnant; 1,200 users have signed up, but you've lost exactly that amount due to churn. This is a very common situation for many businesses, as month-one churn rates are often surprisingly high for

FIGURE 10-1

Customer churn over one year

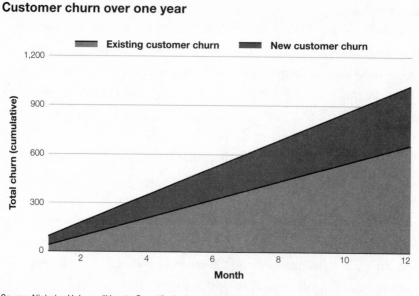

Source: Nicholas Holmes, "How to Quantify the Impact of User Onboarding on Churn and LTV," Nickelled, September 9, 2016, https://www.nickelled.com/blog/how-to-quantify-the-impact-of-user-onboarding-on -churn-and-customer-ltv/. Used with permission of Nicholas Holmes.

software-as-a-service businesses but are often masked as "trials" or "pre-sales accounts" and excluded from calculations. They shouldn't be.

Now, assume your company deploys an onboarding tactic to improve the user experience and increase retention, changing these numbers. If we can bring 70 percent of users back in the first month rather than 50 percent, we'll assume that brings down the new customer churn from 50 percent to 30 percent. And the growth now looks very different.

In total, the business has grown revenues by 18 percent rather than stagnating (see figure 10-2). Now with a decreased churn rate of 7 percent, customers will stay for an average of fourteen months instead of ten months before they churn. So the lifetime customer value has instantly increased, and the bottom line of the business is dramatically affected via marketing's involvement with adoption of the product, not just connecting people to it. In a *Harvard Business Review* article published in the early 2000s, Frederick F. Reichheld and Phil Schefter agreed with that type of growth strategy: they found that increasing customer retention rates by 5 percent

FIGURE 10-2

Reduced churn drives business growth

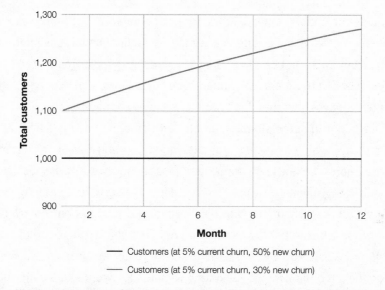

Source: Nicholas Holmes, "How to Quantify the Impact of User Onboarding on Churn and LTV," Nickelled, September 9, 2016, https://www.nickelled.com/blog/how-to-quantify-the-impact-of-user-onboarding-on -churn-and-customer-ltv/. Used with permission of Nicholas Holmes.

increases profits by 25 to 95 percent. The reason high performers are using this trigger is clear.[8]

In the 2016 *State of Marketing* study, we found high-performing marketing organizations to be ten times more likely to use onboarding programs than their underperforming counterparts.[9] Helping people know what to do, when to do it, and how to do it greatly increases the use of the brand and creates a personalized experience for the user. Such triggers are highly effective at increasing adoption and growing revenue in a new way.

Onboarding is a tactical way to help people find value faster, and clearly it has a major impact on the growth of a brand. Beyond onboarding, the customer journey continues along many other points—moments when your customers are going to get stuck, need support, and ask more questions. We've covered the organic need to answer questions to drive demand, and the same holds true for driving a better customer experience

Starting Small and Growing with Confidence

Because the important work of meeting consumers at the right place and time during their journeys can be complex, smaller businesses might shy away from such tactics (like using triggers) in favor of more traditional strategies. But there are ways businesses of any size can join the context marketing revolution that don't require massive changes.

First identify some simple moments. If you don't have the time or resources to conduct full-scale customer interviews and map out a customer journey, you still likely know some basic places you should be. For local businesses, geographical searches are obvious. Consumers searching "food near me" or "car repair near me" are likely to be significant natural triggers for any local businesses, and they are only growing stronger by the day. Work to make sure your brand is there, able to guide next steps. You can easily do this by optimizing your existing website, keywords, and content for that moment so you can leverage it to its fullest.

For many brands this will simply mean owning your social business profiles. This will allow you to manage the basic information about your business, including days and times you are open and your reviews, and augment it with images and coupons. All channels—Yelp, Google, Bing—allow business owners to create a business listing where they can manage the basic information and upload coupons, post news events, and even announce calls to action for booking, buying, ordering, and creating a reservation. By combining these calls to action, you're creating a natural trigger, making it is easy for people to take the next step in their journey.

Beyond being found, you also need to be an active part of your community. This is easily done with social media. If you are a local business, make sure you join the local community groups and that you're consistently engaging in relevant topics. These hyperlocal groups, such as neighborhood groups, often have a significant influence over their population.

For brands that aren't local, you still need to create and foster community and even work with their audiences to build your products. The small, independent clothing line Seamly.co works with its audience to design its clothes. The company does this across multiple channels, including its website and social media channels, mostly Instagram.

For brands just starting up, you must become a member of the community you plan to sell to, long before you start the business. Engage the community, find out what it wants in a neighbor and in a product, and build relationships with its members. Become a vibrant part of the community, and it will want to buy from you.

Extending the value of each customer along his or her journey is also easily done for small businesses, and where local businesses can have an advantage. A personal relationship is a massive driver for repeat purchases, and local businesses can easily build those deep personal relationships. The owners of small businesses tend to be passionate and purpose driven. You don't open a skate shop unless you are passionate about skating, and the same holds true for flowers, hair, and food. Make sure you get to know each person, adding personal touches along the person's journey and sharing your joy with him or her. Handwritten notes telling the person about the product and how it was made or just saying thank you go a long way. These notes can be written in advance and simply added to any order.

After the purchase, a note can be sent as well, even digitally—just a simple and personal check-in to see how things are going. Have they had a chance to use the product? Do they need to make a return? These are simple things you can ask. The goal of the follow-up isn't to sell them more, but rather to show you care and are focused on their needs. Such total experiences can also be automated very inexpensively, because most modern marketing software allows you to send triggered and timed communication.

---

throughout the journey. Brands must include the user/product experience as a part of their purview, triggering experiences along the way that help customers achieve their goal in the moment. Providing a better customer experience not only increases lifetime value; it also moves customers one step closer to advocacy.

While thus far we've focused mostly on how to scale up strategies such as using triggers, note that all these ideas can also be scaled down to busi-

Finally, use advocates to ensure a continuation of the experience. For small businesses, reviews are a powerful driver, and you should ask customers who have great experiences to leave a review. When and how you do that is up to you, but you must ask. Additionally, being a member of your community and creating advocates can be easily done via social media too. My local bike shop takes a picture of each new bike and owner and posts to its social media account. Again, this is such a powerful action because the person buying the product wants to become that thing. You buy a bike because you want to be a cyclist. The validation from a bike shop showcasing you is then validation for this desire, creating a deeper brand relationship through context.

Context-based marketing may seem complex and large, and it can be for those brands that have large and complex scenarios. It can also be made very simple for brands with simple scenarios, such as a local business, by doing three simple things. First, focus on the main aspects of identifying key points along your customers' journey, making sure you are in them and leveraging them. Second, work with your audience either by being an active part of your community or by finding ways to cocreate your products with them, or better yet, both. Finally, focus on creating a great customer experience at every step and turning customers into advocates, keeping the cycle turning. The more of these elements a business can incorporate, the more reliable and sustainable the business will become.

nesses of any size. See the sidebar "Starting Small and Growing with Confidence."

Leveraging the Power of Your Advocates

Word of mouth is perhaps the most trusted form of marketing. In the infinite era, advocacy marketing unleashes opinions and shared experiences that might otherwise sit silent. It also marks the new ultimate goal for context marketers, because the customer journey no longer ends with the purchase.

Brand advocates come in two forms: customers and fans. Both are valuable, and both are needed. The key to creating both is to discover places where people have a passion for what your brand is doing, and leverage those individuals to keep the contextual cycle turning. That passion might result from how your brand has expressed its purpose, the specific features of your product, or the transformation your experience helps them achieve. (See chapter 8, which covers the context framework element purposeful.) Note that advocacy can happen before or after purchase. I've put it last in the new customer journey, but by no means is it limited to postpurchase. Any member of your audience can join your contextual marketing river in the advocacy stage.

Once again, the watchmaker Daniel Wellington offers a great example. Already killing it in the awareness stage with its outstanding and consistent approach, DW also represents best-of-breed in advocacy. To turn its ever-growing audience into advocates, DW awards one person each day with the #DWPickoftheDay (see figure 10-3).

With such an enthusiastic, active audience, it wasn't difficult to trigger followers of DW to become advocates. The company just needed to ask. It asked their fans to begin posting their own images in hopes of being chosen. Entering the daily contest is easy: anyone with a DW watch can take an artistic picture of it (not unlike the influencers do) and tag it with #DanielWellington. Thus DW's ability to foster and leverage advocacy has been off-the-charts successful: over the past six years, fans and influencers combined have posted more than *1.9 million* posts featuring the hashtag. Given that the brand posts slightly fewer than two posts per day, on average, that means 99.9 percent of all hashtags featuring the DW brand have come from its paid and unpaid advocates. That's how advocacy contributes to a constantly flowing effort.

Brands can use many kinds of targeted triggers to create new advocates, and then engage them to keep the cycle flowing. To create new advocates, use a trigger to ask your best customers, in real time, to take an action on

FIGURE 10-3

Source: Danielle Wellington Instagram feed.

your behalf—such as leaving a review—or prompt them to join your community. If you have a digital product, the trigger might pop up as a chatbot, notification, or different offer. If your solution is offline you might trigger people via email, personal outreach, or text.

The key to using targeted triggers is timing. But how do you determine that timing? It depends on the value the customer-advocate seeks, and since the individual is already a customer, this should be pretty obvious. If you're a roofer and your customer is gushing about how happy he is with your work and how well you cleaned up after the job, pull out your tablet and open it directly to the place you want the person to leave a review. Ask if he'd like to make his excitement public for others to find. If your solution is more complex, you might take a different approach.

If your brand has a tool or solution where you can track individual performance, learn to use this as the data to trigger an action. Reporting features can help. For example, you see that some of your customers are getting amazing results with your product, so you reach out and ask them to write a blog post on how they're achieving those results. In the same vein, the next time that customers who are heavy users of your tool log in, congratulate them on their use and invite them to join the community or leave a review.

————————

In every stage of the customer journey, context marketing demands that we rethink execution. We no longer fill a funnel with leads. Our job is to engender a deep understanding of our audience and use triggers to meet them along their journey and break through in context to usher individuals from one moment to the next. This is how we motivate the modern buyer and build modern brands—guiding them from step to step along their journey—regardless of the size or market. Along with rethinking what marketing looks like along the journey, we must rethink how we scale a continuous flow of experiences.

As we'll see in the next chapter, contextual marketers must learn to leverage complex systems of data, technology, and automated programs to move beyond executing campaigns to engineering flowing rivers of demand.

11.

Using Automation to Guide Journeys

Now that you've mapped out customer journeys of your various buyer personas and understand how to use triggers to meet buyers where they are and move them forward, it's time to put those ideas into practice *at scale*. As I've mentioned, none of the concepts I've described so far are easy to implement. But technology can help by creating a strong enough current to carry customers through their journey, stage by stage. Such levels of individualized context require a new form of technology able to instantly create and execute programs in real time: automation.

Marketing automation platforms aren't new. But despite being around for more than twenty years, only 44 percent of brands currently use them.[1] With hundreds of automation tools now available to meet any price point for any kind of company—and the expansive list of positive results—overconfidence in limited media era methods is the only way to explain why companies have failed to adopt automation. But whether it's today or tomorrow, all brands will have to make the shift to automated technology, even the very smallest of businesses. The numerous experiences brands must create are possible only through automation, shifting all brands' creative efforts into a new realm: engineering.

Engineering a system of experiences requires embracing new tactics (or old tactics used in new ways) and investing in a set of connected tools that I call a *contextual platform*. When these connected tools share data, you can automatically reach the highest context in every moment—and guide prospects and customers to the next stage of their journey. Do that, and you will have mastered context marketing.

Crafting Journeys that Flow

A contextual platform absolutely *demands* that every technology across the organization cooperate so that data can be managed to create a composite picture of every prospect and current customer. This cohesive set of technology solutions not only connects every experience across the customer life cycle, but it also leverages the data gathered from each one. The platform's excellent cross communication of data is what powers the granular automations needed to accommodate the many different series of automated personalized experiences. Within each of these separate "currents" in your river, individuals progress in the step order and speed that makes sense for their personal circumstances. Automation is key to keeping your currents strong and moving as many customers forward as possible.

The technologies that make up a contextual platform will be familiar to you, but again, you must rethink how you use them. Most brands currently function under a traditional departmental setup, in which each tool, channel, and internal department operates in its own silo. Because the various tools used by different departments cannot easily share data, there's no chance to leverage that data to trigger brand experiences along the entire customer journey. Reporting is piecemeal, which leads to multiple views of a single customer. Such fragmentation is bad enough within the organization—but worse still, it means that customers receive an incoherent series of brand experiences that undo all your attempts to meet them in context.

For example, a potential customer in the consideration stage might engage with the website, digging deeply into the product and features he or she is interested in. While on the site, the individual also gave permission to receive emails. Next the brand sends an email, yet all the brand knows is that the individual is interested in the brand—not specifically what aspect. So the brand crafts an email about its newest products (what the *brand* wants to talk about) and sends it to the full email list. But even though the customer has shown interest in the brand, in the infinite media era that email is dead on arrival.

For a brand with a contextual platform, all the data is combined, allowing for each experience (in this case email) to be hyperpersonal, showcasing the products the individual is interested in. Recall from an earlier chapter how Room & Board combined data from many places (website, email, purchase history) to make all experiences better. The website presented a contextual experience, and each email was highly context-based on each person's combined individual engagement. Those resulting experiences broke through, driving a 50 percent increase in sales in the first month alone.

A brand leveraging a contextual platform not only can connect the dots but also can open up new marketing possibilities. Where the brand with a siloed journey can send an email to everyone (mass or segmented), the contextual platform can create a personal moment for a single person, based on his or her individual interactions along the entire journey. And because all of the tools and channels are connected, the brand could go ever further by creating a series of experiences deployed across any channel.

You can see this in figure 11-1. On the left side of the figure, the brand has invested in all of the required technology to create an experience in each department. However, the tools are not connected, so there are seven views of the customer (each tool—email, website, social, CRM, backend, service, and community—has its own view). On the right side, you see the opposite: a platform with a single view of the customer. In addition to the way the tools are interconnected, a shared layer of automation allows for any experience at any time to be as contextual as possible. Brands leveraging a contextual platform are not just gaining greater efficiency by consolidation; they are radically increasing the power of the marketing capabilities and opening up new marketing possibilities.

In context marketing, all experiences, data sources, and technologies are connected in a contextual platform, with three defining qualities:

1. All experiences are connected to outcomes.

2. Data is connected and flows freely between applications.

FIGURE 11-1

Siloed technology stack vs. interconnected platform

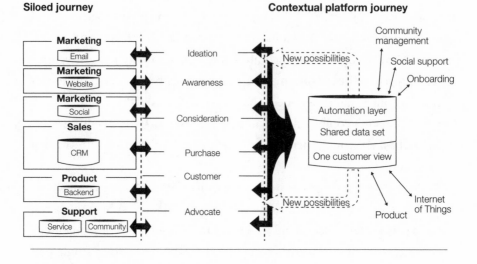

3. The automation layer enables greater context along the customer journey.

The fact is that data interconnectivity isn't optional in the infinite media era. If your tools aren't able to connect easily via an app store, you'll need to invest in new tools or build a platform from scratch, using application protocol interfaces (APIs) to dictate which data can be connected and how. With a connected system that allows data sharing and customer outreach to work in concert, your brand can deliver a seamless experience to every prospect and customer, which has a direct effect on your revenue.

Although the tools that make up your contextual platform will vary by business, you'll need a minimum of five tools to create the platform:

1. CRM (customer relationship management, which is your customer database)

2. Website

3. Product

4. Marketing execution

5. Customer support

Those five tools could represent an investment of anywhere from hundreds of dollars per month for small businesses to tens of thousands per month for larger enterprises. That's why support and buy-in from company leadership is so critical. And those are just the five *essential* tools. I've seen brands using up to thirty-nine tools, though according to Salesforce's 2017 *State of Marketing* study, high-performing marketing organizations on average use a combination of fourteen tools to create a cohesive customer journey.[2] The number of tools isn't the important part; it is how well they're connected that makes the difference.

Let's look at a few examples. Craveable Brands, the Australian group of 570 quick-serve restaurants, including the brands Oporto, Red Rooster, and Chicken Treat, connects its in-store ordering systems with its marketing systems to make it easier to identify and retain loyal customers. Its most recent success was leveraging the customer data and permission gained in the stores' point-of-sale system to onboard customers via short message service (SMS) to a new online delivery service. That move alone produced an additional $9 million in online sales. Ken Russell, the company's head of digital marketing and strategy, commented on that recent success: "We want our brands to be Australia's best known and most loved restaurant brands. The customer experience across all channels is vital—not just in-store."[3]

A contextual platform also links demand generation to a complete view of the sales and marketing pipeline. All progress made in the customer journeys of individuals can be measured and automated across the organization. For example, Associa, a large US property management firm, uses its contextual platform to automate lead nurturing and provide sales teams insights into their prospects in real time. As a result, marketing is able to create more leads, and sales can track prospects' interaction with marketing collateral, allowing them to focus on the most sales-ready opportunities. Matt Kraft, SVP of marketing and sales at Associa, says the combined effort produced a 40 percent increase in sales.[4]

Harnessing Automated Programs to Meet Your Goals

Automations are a relatively new topic in marketing, and many marketers have little experience with even basic automations. But such programs are the connective tissue between contextual experiences. Therefore we'll examine in this section the basic premise of an automation and how contextual experiences connect to become automated programs. We'll also look at more advanced possibilities of what can be automated.

All of this means that when you begin to design your automations, you'll need to think as an engineer does. Automations are complex systems, requiring a different approach from typical marketing procedures. To get us all on the same page, provide you with that new approach, and demonstrate how automations can scale contextual experiences across the journey, I'll cover six things you should consider when working with automated programs.

Keep Multiple Triggers Firing

Automated programs challenge marketers to think differently: it's no longer a brilliant advertising concept with copy written to convert the unsuspecting masses into customers; the creativity is in how to leverage the data and the technology to reliably, and repeatably, create the perfect experience for each person in any moment. Learning to shift your thinking to these very granular experiences means thinking in Boolean logic, which, in short, means the following: IF this happens, THEN do this. Such as, IF a prospect has not returned to the website within thirty days, THEN send an email. This is a targeted trigger sent by the brand in response to a consumer's action, or lack thereof. The logic is composed of three parts: commands, a trigger, and function(s).

There are, of course, many commands that can be combined to create very specific automations, creating an extended network of triggers firing for each person at the exact moment, in real time. Your platform and its tools will determine exactly which specific commands and programs are possible. Here's the general type of data each tool of the "bare minimum" set provides:

1. CRM—sales engagement and purchase history data

2. Website—page views, number of visits, search terms, and content engagement data

3. Product—product usage data

4. Marketing execution—marketing engagement data (email opens, chatbot conversations, link clicks, video plays, content downloads)

5. Customer support—when, what, level and type of issue, resolution

A single program, as seen in figure 11-2, may have eighteen or more different lines of logic, which read more like a decision tree than lines of code. These types of automated programs turn each trickling journey you start into a strong flow of demand.

The more data you can connect among the tools in your contextual platform, the more creative you can be with how your automated programs are triggered, and where and when you can initiate or guide individuals to the next stage of their customer journey.

Create Triggers for Next-Stage Content

Automated programs move individuals forward (or "downriver" if that's how you think of the journey), but to do so, they must (1) be able to identify the prospect's/customer's current stage of the journey, (2) be capable of reading an individual's specific activity, and (3) be able to deliver the appropriate experience that will guide that prospect/customer to the next step.

The easiest way to determine the stage of the journey is by observing a direct action a person takes. That's because people will only engage with what is contextual, so if they are engaging, they are telling you where on the journey they are—that is, if you mapped your content to your journey. Such knowledge is key to motivating them to take the next steps. Let's say someone engages with a "best of" list you have published to your blog. Once

FIGURE 11-2

Using an automated program to nurture customer reengagement

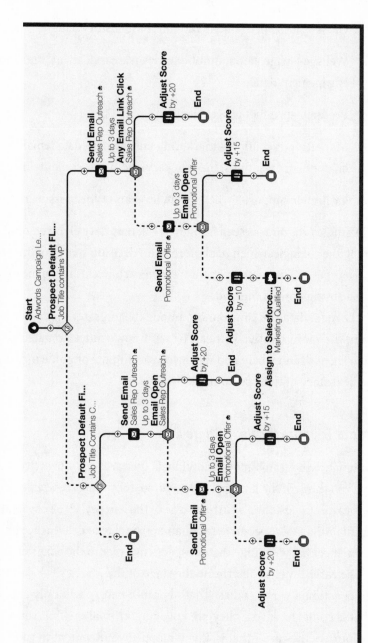

she has opened that article, your automated program might suggest two more pieces of content for her in a sidebar or at the bottom of the web page. The first suggestion should be another piece of content designed for the stage she's in, and the second should answer a question in the next stage. Thus you are able to fulfill her current needs while also guiding her to move to the next question she needs to ask. The motivation to move forward is her idea—you just made the step easy to take.

With high-consideration purchases, you'll automate programs that collect information in a way that looks much like lead scoring—a technique of assigning points to an individual based on the person's specific attributes measuring intent—though again, you will be using it in a new way. Rather than gathering a user's demographic data, such as job title, industry, budget, and timeline (measures of how interested you are in the user), you'll ask a program to measure how many times the person has engaged in content tailored for the awareness stage and use that to measure the person's *interest in you*. In this way, lead scoring becomes a new data point used by programs to measure current interest, triggering a wide range of possibilities.

For example, you might have an automated program giving individuals five points for each engagement with awareness content; once their score reaches fifteen or more, an automated program sends each person an invitation to a webinar targeted for prospects in the consideration stage. Similarly, a person who has built up a lead score of 100 points might automatically receive a human-to-human brand experience—outreach by a sales rep, perhaps—aligning marketing and sales into a seamless process.

Lead scoring is a critical data point for contextual marketing. If this is something your brand has always left to the sales team, there's an easy way for you to get started: look at the past ten closed deals for each persona in your map and the series of actions leading up to the sale. Now that your tools are all connected, you should have access to this data. Next, divide the number of actions into the stages of the customer journey to arrive at your sales-ready score.

I suggest using 100 as the *sales-ready score*, the threshold someone must meet before being passed to sales. To illustrate, if you had 20 actions, each action would award 5 points to the individual ($100/20 = 5$). The individual will accumulate points with each engagement, and when the individual reaches 100 he or she will be sales-ready. This basic formula gets you started, and as you pass leads over to sales, work with them to refine your scores into their correct value. Many brands fall short here because they forget lead scoring is a living and breathing program that must be refined over time as products and customer journeys evolve.

Ease the Permissions Process

Permission, in theory, is simple: just ask for it. In practice, however, the theory works best when leveraging contextual methods that are conversational (see chapter 5 for more about permission). At first glance, automations may sound ill suited to the task, but they have proved to help brands gain more permissions to keep your prospects moving downriver.

As we learned in chapter 5, gaining permission to contact people directly is essential to breaking through in context, and one of the most common methods is the value exchange. This method requires consumers to fill out forms with their personal information in exchange for access to useful content, or other form of value, that meets their need or desire of the moment. Requiring someone to fill out a form is something people expect, but that doesn't mean it won't cause them to bail at the last minute. You can avoid having people ditch you at the sight of a form and improve your engagement by using "progressive profiling."

Progressive profiling was first proposed in Seth Godin's book *Permission Marketing*, published in 1999. Back then, however, we didn't have the technology to automatically break up the questions over a number of interactions with your brand. For example, your first request might be only for a valid email address. Your next interaction—in response to their request to access a webinar, for example—would require people to give their name, such as in figure 11-3.

A strong contextual platform has a single, 360-degree view of the customer at all times, so it can make progressive profiling happen across channels. For example, a first interaction on a social channel asks for the email, then a subsequent visit to your website asks for their name. The progressive nature of the experience ensures that you aren't asking them to type in the same information repeatedly.

FIGURE 11-3

Example of progressive profiling

FIGURE 11-4

Using a chatbot to gain permission

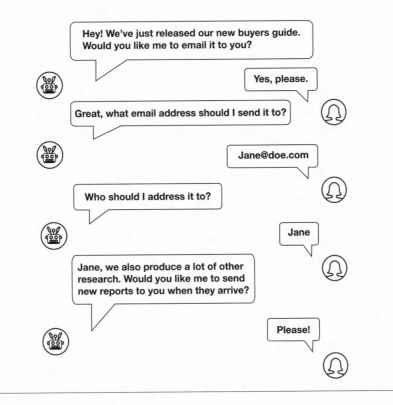

You can ease permission requests using a chatbot. More advanced marketers have already begun to use chatbots to gain the required permission information via conversation while on the website—instead of using a form. Figure 11-4 provides an example of how that might look.

Chatbots can be triggered to pop up at any time on different channels. They can be deployed on websites to gain email permission, as the figure shows, or they can be used to expand permissions to social media channels, such as using a Facebook Messenger bot to communicate directly with your social audience, which you can then cross-pollinate to grow your email audience.

The other great news about chatbots is that *people like them*. They are conversational, are efficient at getting to the point (the good ones, at least), and eliminate the irritating task of filling out forms. Segment.io, an enterprise software vendor, uses chatbots to gain permission on its website and has seen a fivefold increase in engagement and a twofold increase in conversions.[5]

Scale Personal Customer Journeys

Most customers pause at some point along their journeys and don't interact with your brand. Yet as a brand, you must be ready to meet your prospects and customers the moment they reengage, as if no time has passed. In other words, brand experiences must be connected experiences. Automated programs provide the power to scale thousands of such connected, personal currents, as seen in figure 11-5 for a hypothetical clothing company.

From its customer research interviews, this brand knows visitors to its adventure clothing section are most likely in the process of planning a trip. They feel excited about the trip, and if it is a new sport or a new location, a little nervous too. Customers are hungry for content that will answer their questions and offer a picture of what to expect when they arrive at their destination. Fulfill those desires, and your brand can simultaneously feed customers' excitement and ease their anxiety. In figure 11-5, this brand has programmed a vast network of possible actions to keep various currents flowing in the purchase stage of the customer journey. Each experience is triggered to just a single individual and only when the correct conditions apply.

In this low-consideration scenario (i.e., a low-cost product compared with, say, a computer), the brand begins by asking whether the visitor added an item to a shopping cart. If yes, then the obvious work is to find out why that item has not been purchased. If no item has been selected, then

FIGURE 11-5

Automated programs keep things moving during and after the purchase stage

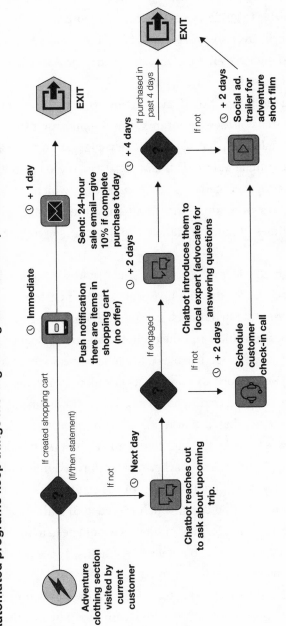

Adventure clothing section visited by current customer

(if/then statement)

If created shopping cart

⊘ Immediate

Push notification there are items in shopping cart (no offer)

⊘ + 1 day

Send: 24-hour sale email—give 10% if complete purchase today

EXIT

If not

⊘ Next day

Chatbot reaches out to ask about upcoming trip.

If engaged

⊘ + 2 days

Chatbot introduces them to local expert (advocate) for answering questions

⊘ + 4 days

If purchased in past 4 days

EXIT

If not

⊘ + 2 days

Schedule customer check-in call

If not

⊘ + 2 days

Social ad. trailer for adventure short film

EXIT

content must nurture the visitor's interest in the items viewed. With this visual flowchart, you can see how the flow of the current is dependent on automated technology to scale purchases. Without this level of targeting, it's impossible to guide customers toward their desired outcome in context. Precise decisions on when to use ads, where the ads take them, and what content to offer are all done at scale to carry prospects along the journey, moment to moment.

Where the automation depicted above is a single program, brands can have hundreds of these programs running, meaning there are situations where a single prospect may be actively engaged in more than one automated program at a time. This complexity is solved by another simple automated program called a *frequency cap*, which introduces global rules—across programs—that limit the number of exposures, experiences, or times a brand reaches out to a single person over a certain number of days.

For high-consideration products and services, automated programs are just as essential for moving prospects through customer journeys—and they can produce rapid results, and for any industry. A great example comes from higher education and the online school of an Ivy League university. The prestigious school, listed as a top ten business school by *U.S. News & World Report*, needed to improve its enrollment numbers. Its marketing team had exhausted traditional marketing methods, and after being introduced to context-based marketing, they decided to implement it. Their first step was to make the case to the university's leadership to invest in a contextual platform. The marketing team proved it would cost less than $50,000 per year—a small fraction of the university's annual investment in current advertising costs, which exceeded $1 million at the time. This implied that the new form of marketing would need to improve the enrollment rate by only a fraction of a percent to justify the investment. Unsurprisingly, their request was granted.

The university's marketing team followed the steps outlined in this book and shared their story with me. The team began by identifying the stages and personas of the customer journey by undertaking detailed interviews. Using the results, they mapped journeys for each college course, setting up triggers for each relevant search term to capture prospective students in the exact moment they were looking to learn more. By delivering strong content, the prestigious university gained permission to contact interested students directly.

Next, the automated programs took over, identifying each person's stage in the journey based on the moment the individual entered. Guided by each individual's cumulative interactions (tracked as their lead score), the program then delivered a series of direct email communications helping guide prospective students along their journey. The higher the score, the more sales-ready content the programs would deliver. The emails delivering the experiences were crafted in rich text, with a look and feel similar to personal email correspondence; the marketing team adopted a conversational tone as well, allowing the brand experience to reach high levels of context.

Every interaction and data point was fed back into the contextual platform, where another program was waiting to fire off content, testimonials, or video links during the consideration stage. Once the individual's lead score reached the sales-ready threshold (= 100), another program would alert an enrollment representative from the university to reach out (human-to-human) to guide the student through the enrollment process.

A comparison of the school's traditional campaign results with those achieved through contextual marketing makes the difference in outcomes clear:

- **Traditional campaign:** Using a paid search campaign powered by Google AdWords (now GoogleAds), the university drove prospects to a landing page to receive information about a course. Of those who landed on the page, 7 percent converted into sales qualified leads, and of those sales qualified leads, 3 percent converted into students. For every one hundred people, 0.02 percent became a student, meaning the campaign needed to reach five hundred people to equal one enrolled student.

- **Contextual program:** The contextual program was run on thirty thousand new and incumbent prospects. Of those thirty thousand, 18 percent converted into a sales qualified lead, and of those sales qualified leads, 50 percent converted into students. So, for every one hundred people exposed to the program, nine became students. To put this on equal terms with the traditional campaign: every five hundred people exposed to the contextual program produced forty students—generating forty times the revenue of the traditional campaign.

Close the Sale

Late-stage buyers who have yet to move to the purchase stage can also be guided using automated programs. Whether it's an email with an additional discount or a message reminding them of the items left in their cart, automations can help close the purchase. Taking this idea a step further, during the 2017 holiday season, Lego connected its online shopping experience with a chatbot, named Ralph, on social media to create an extremely contextual brand experience designed especially for late-stage buyers.[6]

Ralph was designed to help people find the best Lego gift possible, which can be difficult since Lego has such an enormous product catalog. Ralph operated within Facebook Messenger, moving him much closer in context than an ad or email ever could. To put Ralph in play, Lego used its tracking data on all visitors to the Lego website and created a program triggered to communicate only with people who had (1) visited the site in the past fourteen days; and (2) had not bought anything in the prior seven days. This program required a connected platform able to gather the required information across Lego's website and ordering system, then used it to produce an experience within Facebook.

Once people who met the criteria logged on to Facebook, they received an ad from Lego—a great example of how advertising can be part of a larger journey. The ad wasn't designed to drive people back to Lego's site but rather to invite them into a conversation on Facebook Messenger with Ralph, the chatbot (see figure 11-6).

The program that drove Ralph's conversation was designed to guide each consumer through a series of questions that progressively filled in a profile of the person who would be receiving the Lego gift. This information allowed Ralph to offer the most suitable Lego set—all in a "conversation" that lasted, on average, about four minutes.

FIGURE 11-6

Source: 1) Lego website; 2) https://www.facebook.com/business/success/2-lego; 3) https://mobilemarketingmagazine.com/lego-ralph-chatbot-facebook-messenger-news-feed-christmas.

The entire automated program that powered Ralph ran seamlessly across the Lego website, Facebook advertising, and Facebook Messenger, closing sales at scale while staying in close context with each individual shopper. To be clear, the sale happened *during the chat*. Ralph helped buyers find the best gifts and allowed them to make a purchase without ever leaving Facebook Messenger. The experience was connected in an entirely new way, and purchases made through Ralph were 1.9 times higher than average orders on the Lego site (non–bot assisted). Even more outstanding: this single automated program accounted for 25 percent of Lego's 2017 in-season, annual online sales.[7]

Increase Lifetime Customer Value

On top of everything else, automation goes a long way toward keeping communication with existing customers alive and increasing lifetime customer value (LCV). Ultimately that means guiding customers toward advocacy for your brand—a stage that often gets overlooked, especially if your marketing team is still stuck in "filling the funnel" mode. Postpurchase automation programs stay on top of repeat purchases and drive the customer retention needed to keep company performance strong and numbers growing.

Salesforce uses automation to onboard thousands of new customers each quarter, providing those individuals everything they need to become a super-user of our services and an advocate for our brand. The program starts with an automated welcome email that contains two calls to action (CTA): a primary action (register for a webinar) and a secondary action (join the Success Community). The primary CTA offers registration for a free "Welcome to Salesforce" webinar, while further down in the email, the secondary CTA offers membership in our Trailblazer Community. These emails are dynamic: the next automated program will send an experience based on the recipient's engagement (or lack thereof) with the first. For example, if the person attended the most recently recommended webinar, the program will follow up with the next webinar in the series. If the person didn't attend, the program will customize a message to encourage him or her to do so.

In the weeks following the welcome email, new customers will continue to receive a series of emails pointing them to increasingly advanced webinars, as well as other supportive resources, such as videos and walk-throughs. Each communication guides customers deeper into all the functionality that Salesforce offers. If engaged with the content and deployment is going well, these newer customers continue hearing from our Success Services team for a month, or until they are up and running successfully on our platform. Eventually they are put on another automated program to expand their use of our products and solutions.

If the program detects low engagement, as well as low usage patterns with the product, the individual is sent on a different journey, with content designed to break through contextually (for example, in moments of frustration). If that doesn't rectify the issue, a case is automatically created and assigned to a customer success manager who reaches out to help (human-to-human). These programs have proved to be highly effective: customers who complete the onboarding program and join the Trailblazer Community (including Trailhead) buy, on average, twice as many Salesforce products and services and remain customers four times as long, producing significant overall increases for Salesforce in user adoption and LCV.

Next: Decentralize Your Automated Programs

Once you've embraced the power of automations, you can start moving toward what comes next in the infinite era: decentralized automation.

While each tool is capable of automations, such as using your marketing automation platform to send email or your website to change content, they are centralized tools—meaning they ingest data, process that data, and execute on that data. Everything they do happens within the walls of that tool. But decentralized automations happen *across a network of tools*, expanding the total possibilities of experiences. That's one of the keys to how Airbnb grew so quickly—and how a new idea of automations will fuel future brand experiences.

When the company was getting started, Airbnb identified the moments where its audiences were naturally engaging. It had two audiences: people looking to rent out their place (host), and people looking to rent a place (consumer). It found those audiences—and the right moment to approach them—on Craigslist. Reaching them at scale meant creating automations. Following the context framework, it leveraged the elements of available, personal, permission, and authentic to break through.

To reach its first audience, hosts, Airbnb leveraged the native communication channel for the Craigslist website: email. Creating an automation that would find each new Craigslist posting for a place to rent, pull data from it, and create a highly personal email sent directly to the person who posted—that's a targeted trigger. Here's one of those actual emails:[8]

> I'm emailing you because you have one of the nicest listings on Craigslist in the Tahoe area, and I wanted to recommend you feature it on one of the largest vacation rental marketplaces on the web, AirBnB. The site already has 3,000,000 page views per month. Check it out here (URL to AirBnB).
>
> Jill D.

The permission was assumed, and the message highly authentic. It was written as a person would write it, even being signed by a person, "Jill D."

This simple automation is what brought so many people to Airbnb, and was the trigger to get them to list their spaces on the new site. Now Airbnb had to get those listings rented out. To accomplish that, it created another automation, in reverse. The company automatically reposted all Airbnb listings *back onto Craigslist*, effectively introducing a natural moment found on the customer journey, while helping customers achieve their goal at the moment, which was to find the best place to rent.

Note that Airbnb didn't create either of those automations using just one single tool. Rather, it used a combination of tools, pulling data from different sources and using different tools for execution. That's decentralized automation.

But while the Airbnb example is very simplistic, today context marketers are leveraging decentralized automations in a way that's far from simple. In the infinite era, we all need to understand that automations are already integrated into every tool your business uses. Your sales tools can automate emails, your chatbot tool can automate conversations, and your website can automatically change its content to meet the individual in the moment. Learning to combine these automations is the next step to creating even more contextual experiences.

For example, your product may already have a feed of data telling you what consumers are using and how they are using it. Accessing that data isn't possible using a standard marketing automation tool, which is why a wave of technologies have entered the scene, allowing marketers to easily access backend data without having to involve engineers. These tools create a feed of data that other tools can leverage to transform into the information you need for your automations to operate when and how they should.

Now imagine you put a new feature in your product and want to ask your customers how they feel about it. In real time, the data directs another tool to deploy a survey asking about the feature. The results of that survey become fresh data telling you who is happy and who isn't—data that can then be leveraged the next time a customer arrives (for example, "If the survey score is 8 or greater, do X; if it is lower than 8, do Y"). That could mean either popping up a chatbot that shows the customer how to get value from the new feature or, for those super happy customers, asking them to leave a review. Again, note that this string of experiences happens across many tools, yet does not include a traditional marketing automation platform.

Brands in the infinite media era must begin to see automations as the future of experiences, and realize that to create them, they'll need to connect all tools and data together. This is why a platform is so critical. Marketing automation tools are a major piece of that platform. But automations won't be happening only in traditional marketing execution. Automations will be everywhere along the customer journey, and for good reason. As brands begin to shift to contextual methods and embrace a customer journey strategy, put a platform of context in place, and begin to set up and manage a myriad of automations across them, the next radical shift becomes apparent. The increased requirements of the marketing department far exceed our current processes of working. Even with automations, there simply isn't enough time in the day to do it all, which is why high-performing marketing organizations have embraced a new way of working that allows them to not only manage the chaos but also produce the highest level of value per unit of time. High performers embrace the *agile method*.

12.

Faster, Better

Building Agile Processes into the Journey

During Twitter's glory days of massive growth from 2010 to 2012, the company wasn't doing anything drastic to produce the results it was seeing. It didn't advertise more or increase its media coverage or improve its branding. In fact, it changed only one thing in its growth model: it simply ran more tests. This is the revelation Satya Patel, former VP of product at Twitter, shared at the 2014 Agile Marketing Meetup.[1] Beginning in the first quarter of 2011, Twitter began running *ten* tests each week, up from one every two weeks. This "rapid experimentation" allowed the company to find the experiences and techniques its customers were wanting and to trigger those experiences at opportune times. The result? Twitter grew faster than ever before (see figure 12-1).

In their book *Hacking Growth*, Morgan Brown and Sean Ellis view such rapid experimentation, or High Tempo Testing as they call it, as the epitome of modern creativity—and key to helping companies move ahead. Besides Twitter, the authors look at companies like Facebook, Uber, Dropbox, and Airbnb, peeling back the layers to explain their explosive growth. Like Twitter, those companies' success had nothing to do with creative PR campaigns or better use of tactics. Rather, as Brown told me in a recent conversation, "They simply learn faster than all of us."

In other words, scaling your business isn't a matter of coming up with the most creative idea. Instead, it's all about quickly testing assumptions

FIGURE 12-1

Twitter growth, 2010–2012

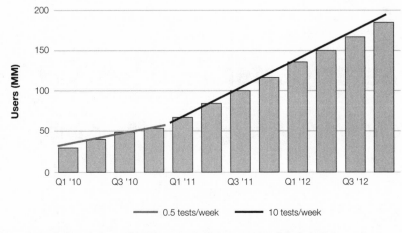

Source: https://agilemarketing.net/high-tempo-testing/?utm_campaign=Submission&utm_medium
=Community&utm_source=GrowthHackers.com. Used with permission of Satya Patel.

to arrive at an optimum result. What's more, you'll need to apply rapid experimentation across the entire customer journey to achieve the best results, because such iterative testing improves any experience. Recall from earlier in the book that even a small improvement in efficiency has a massive impact on revenue—a mere 1 percent increase in efficiency across the first four stages of the journey creates a 40 percent lift in net new revenue. Therefore, we must see the entire customer journey *as an experiment* in which our job isn't to "get creative" but instead to constantly test our assumptions across the journey and improve every day.

The process of rapid testing is called *agile*, and it is a key trait of high-performing marketing organizations. While there are other modern methods for production that sound similar, such as Fail Fast or Lean, they are not the same. Lean is about removing waste from your current production process, and Fail Fast simply refers to taking more risk. Both are improvements to your current methods, while agile is an entirely new process of constant iteration that aligns the brand and the customer. In 2018, the Standish Group found that agile projects succeed two times more often, at a quicker pace, and at a significantly lower cost than projects following the traditional production process.[2] Salesforce research concurs: high performers are ten times more likely to use agile methods than are their underperforming counterparts.[3]

Consider agile as simultaneously a tactical approach, an organizational structure, and a new lens through which to view all things. You will need such a lens, given all that the transition from traditional to contextual marketing practices requires: laying considerable groundwork and maintaining a relentless focus on creating contextual experiences (and all it implies) amid changing consumer demands—*all* while managing hundreds of automated programs that run simultaneously. What's more, the bar for what constitutes a "better" experience for consumers will continually go higher, putting marketers in a very tough spot: we must find a way to consistently produce more experiences at a higher value. Agile is the answer to this problem, and a core skill of the context marketer. (In case your team needs convincing, however, see the sidebar "How to Advocate for the Power of Agile.")

This chapter shows you how to use agile to improve and speed up the customer journey, how to build journeys using data-backed testing, and how to use agile backlogs to stay focused and get the highest return on your effort.

Crafting Better Journeys in Less Time

Agile has many applications, and customer journeys are a big one. Although the people who came up with the idea of agile were software developers trying to create computer programs, agile processes solve the exact same problems for marketers who are crafting an endless mix of experiences. That's because marketers face challenges similar to those of developers. Think about it: developers were separated from their end users; they were trying to build products while having very little context regarding what they were solving; their projects were based on assumption without testing; they were constantly asked to make changes to the deliverable as the projects progressed; and as a result, projects would miss timelines—and not really solve the actual needs of consumers. Sound familiar?

How to Advocate for the Power of Agile

In case you're faced with team members who really can't understand the concept of agile or why they should change the way they create brand experiences, you can show them a very simple proof. It's an example of the power of agile to produce anything—better and faster.

- Take a sheet of paper and draw two dots on opposite corners, like this:

●

●

- Ask team members to replicate your drawing on their own sheets of paper. Then ask them to place their pens on one of the dots, close their eyes, and—without picking up the pen—try to draw a straight line to the other dot. Ask them to stop when they think they've gotten there, and to open their eyes. Let them know they can take their time and can begin when they are ready. When they are finished, their lines will most likely look something like this:

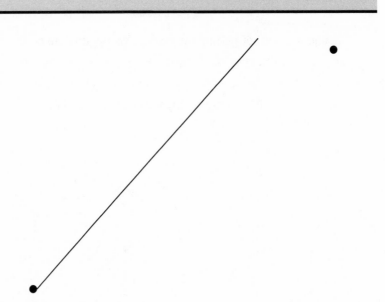

- If they happened to hit the dot, which is rare, you need to show that it was pure luck, not proof that the method is correct. To prove that success using such an approach involves sheer luck, simply ask the team members to use the same method to hit the mark again, three times in a row. The odds are they can't repeat the feat. (The approach they just used mimics what's commonly referred to as the Waterfall method of production, where the full plan is drawn up in advance and then executed in cascade fashion without reflection, such as on an assembly line.)

- Now ask them to try again, but this time following the more iterative process of agile. Ask them to place the pen on the dot, close their eyes, and start drawing—but to stop at any point they wish, keeping the pen on the paper. At that point they should open their eyes and recalibrate (without lifting the pen). Then ask them to close their eyes again, and continue forward. Each of the team members' second lines will likely look like some version of this—more of a zig-zag pattern than a line, but reaching the dot nonetheless:

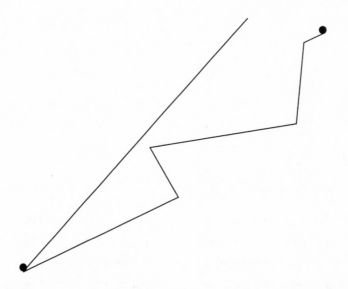

You can repeat the agile exercise as many times as you like, and you'll see that the agile line will *always* reach the mark, faster and with less energy. That's because agile is the only way to reliably create a better experience, and it is scalable.

But then the software developers realized something: the problems they confronted were simply by-products of the *processes* they were following. Their solution? Craft a *new process*—agile. Founded on a core set of principles, agile sought to provide the *why* that outlined the process and the structure. Agile as a process is based on multiple iterations rather than a single attempt, and it values objective feedback over subjective opinions.

FIGURE 12-2

The agile process

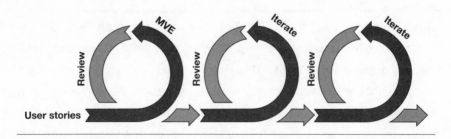

As a structure, agile focuses on collaborative teams rather than siloed channel teams.

We can think of agile processes, therefore, as springing from the structure of the problem itself. How to create the most effective and efficient journey? By involving all parties in a process of collaboration and testing, agile journeys simply produce better outcomes faster. Collaboration happens both internally and externally. Customers are involved at each stage of the building process, where their feedback combined with quantitative results provides the direction for the next iteration. Internally, collaboration is created by a new team structure called a *pod*: a diverse group of skill sets working together to test ideas, gain instant feedback, and iterate to create a better experience. (See the sidebar "Capital One: Case Study of an Agile Team.")

Such teams—pods—follow agile processes, as conceptualized by the image in figure 12-2.

Specifically, the agile process begins with user stories. These stories tell you how the person is naturally engaging across the journey, which is why the first chapter of part three outlined in detail how to obtain those stories (a.k.a., market research). Then the process moves to creating a minimum viable experience (MVE), which the pod crafts as a hypothesis. The MVE is not a finished product or experience; rather, it's only the first test, usually the easiest way to test a basic assumption.

For example, Santander Bank gave up long production schedules and lengthy approval processes to execute a single marketing effort, switching

Capital One: Case Study of an Agile Team

What do Alec Baldwin, Samuel L. Jackson, Seinfeld's dad, and a Viking all have in common? They've all asked you, "What's in your wallet?" That's the well-known catchphrase of Capital One Financial, the progressive credit card company that pioneered new credit models, online banking, mobile banking, and now agile marketing. You may not think of a financial company as being progressive, but this one was founded, in 1988, on that very idea: that the power of information, technology, and testing could be harnessed to bring highly customized financial products directly to consumers.

Indeed, the bank was one of the first companies to put agile to the test on a large scale in a marketing department. Through conversations with past and present unnamed sources familiar with the effort, I was told the organization viewed this as a pivotal business decision. The message to the marketing team was, "We moved to agile, and burned all the boats. There is no turning back." Capital One made the move for a few key reasons. First, it had used agile in other parts of the organization for many years, so it was already a core of the business.[4] Second, the executives saw how divisions outside of technology could benefit from agile as well. They tried out the idea in a very small niche test, watched by management. They liked what they saw and went all in.

As a result, I was told by my source, not only has the quality and speed of marketers' work improved, but also the fundamental way people viewed their work. Agile allowed them to align everyone's goals, and the process supported and reinforced this alignment. Agile helped shift everyone's concept of marketing from subjective to measurable and optimized efforts for the most value per unit of time possible. By reorienting marketing around agile, suddenly the division of 130 people became dynamically responsive to customers' needs.

My sources said the key to the bank marketers' success was how they structured and built the agile teams. To begin, they identified work that could easily be done in an agile format, where multiple iterations were possible. Work such as content creation, digital experiences, and customer journey management are easy places to begin since they allow for rapid deployment and instant feedback. Capital One chose twelve specific teams, almost half of the marketing organization, to produce work in an agile way. (Some teams, such as the Events team, which needed to follow sequential processes, were not moved to agile initially.)

Each of the new teams was renamed as a "pod," and the pods were broken down into four layers, with an accountable executive (AE) at the top, then a project manager (PM), a project owner (PO), and finally the trades. The trades consisted of copy writing, graphic design, art direction, data analysis, and coordination. They were supported by external partnerships, such as channel sales, to support larger business goals.

While the AE determined the team's direction, the PM was in charge of designing the time frame for the project and the objectives the team intended to achieve at each step. The PM answered questions such as the following: What does MVE look like? What will it take to make this happen? Which channels should we use? In what way? The PM and the PO then worked together on a detailed plan, with the PO setting the intent and priority of the outcomes. Next, the project would be decompressed into tasks that were placed into a queue. The PO and the entire pod would then do a forced ranking on those initiatives and break up the work. The team then took the top three things and put those into production. The rest went on the backlog.

The pod used a standard agile process. It began by collecting user stories, moving to a quick production cycle, followed by review and iteration. As a part of the review, the business analyst showed the pod the results, and the pod would fold the findings back into the planning. Sometimes the data might change the order and priority of tasks and move things into or out of the backlog. In addition to reviewing the project, the pod would also look at whether the process used was efficient. So pods were iterating not only their work but also the process of how the work was done.

Each pod was supported in two key ways that allowed it to succeed. First, each had external partnerships, such as key technology administrators and subject matter experts. But more important, each was assigned an agile guide. Since Capital One had already been using agile on the product side, the bank provided its marketing pods with experts in the agile process. These agile experts became internal consultants, aiding the agile teams and the executives to ensure the effort was a success.

Technology and innovation have been the core of Capital One, allowing the company to create variable-interest-rate credit cards before anyone else, and leading it to the fruits of agile marketing. Moreover, the bank's focus on innovation and technology has placed it on InformationWeek's list of the five hundred most innovative users of information technology as well as *Fortune Magazine*'s list of the World's Most Admired Companies, and earned it excellent placements on yearly *Fortune* 500 lists. It is also the ninth-largest bank in the United States. These are massive achievements for a relatively young company, and one in an industry traditionally lacking innovation.

Changing the structure of your entire marketing organization is likely one of the most extreme things you can do. Yet Capital One has demonstrated the necessity today of such radical change—both in how we think about marketing and in how we execute it.

instead to employing many smaller low-risk (MVE) efforts that were quickly launched and measured. Successful efforts were reinvested in and grown, while unsuccessful efforts were abandoned. A case in point is the bank's sponsorship of Boris Bikes—a public bicycle-share company in London. Santander began with a small number of bikes and pickup points. Before deploying new bike stations, the bank sought customer feedback and data— such as, what are the most commonly used bike routes—to decide where and how to best grow the effort. Santander's agile approach across its marketing efforts has led to a 12 percent increase in loyalty and an account satisfaction increase of 10 percent, which is the bank's highest level of customer satisfaction in seventeen years.[5]

Returning to figure 12-2, the MVE is followed by a review of the test, utilizing more customer feedback and quantitative data to determine what the best next steps are, and then the pod iterates again. The power of the agile process comes from that cycle of collaboration and iteration. Such constant feedback, collaboration, and testing allows an idea to reach its highest value every time. By iterating through this process multiple times, you decrease the risk for failure and increase the value of the experience because you are building from the previous learnings.

Data-backed Testing—not Biased Assumptions

Traditionally, marketers follow a customer journey strategy that takes months to carry out. First they diagram on a massive whiteboard the series of steps they envision. They take pictures of it and send those to the brand campaign team to build out. The images reveal the loads of new content that needs to be written, shot, and produced. Then there are accompanying programs to be engineered, landing pages to design, and more.

But even if you've based that campaign on consumer stories and interviews, you are still building it with bias. Just because *you* think your content and brand experiences will work, that doesn't ensure they will. Without testing your assumptions, you're betting a whole lot of time, effort, and money on your own unproven bias.

By contrast, an agile process builds customer journeys in blocks or small steps, where each set of experiences is created and *tested iteratively* until the result is clear—using real data rather than biased guesswork. This process of partial creation and iteration is quicker and much easier to balance with your regular workload. Rather than investing a lot of time to build one big program, you're building one step of a program at a time. That allows you to switch between multiple programs, optimizing each one as you go. The process might look something like figure 12-3.

The first and second actions in the journey are the test—will the customer open the email you sent?—while actions marked as 1, 2, 3 have yet to be built. They will be built in time, using the data gathered from the prior test.

FIGURE 12-3

Creating an automated journey using agile

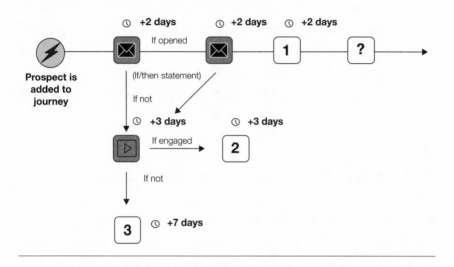

Just how long you have to build the next steps is totally up to you, but use the time between actions as your guide. In this example, the automated program starts out with a two-day pause, meaning a person is added to the program and two days later the first email goes out. The pause in this example is marked with the small clock and a number of days above the action. If the person engages, the program waits two more days before its next action; and if the person does not engage, it waits three days before it takes an alternative action. By adding up the pauses, you can see the brand has six days from when the person first enters the program until the next action (represented as box #1) in the program has to be built, leaving ample time to review and iterate on the first steps.

Following the same logic, the brand has eight days to create the action marked with #2, and twelve days to create action #3. This process continues until the journey is complete, at which point it will have been built over time, and optimized with the data gained from each test, rather than biased guesswork. The result is that you can actually build your brand experiences faster—and achieve better outcomes.

By relying on audience engagement and changes to that engagement over time, any bias on the part of your marketing teams is removed. What bias, you ask? Let me be clear about how *much* bias drives marketing decisions. Ask yourself, when was the last time you picked up the phone to talk to someone who had engaged with your marketing, with the express goal of learning how to make that experience better for the next person?

I've put this question to tens of thousands of marketers from around the globe, and less than 1 percent of marketers have *ever* made such a phone call. Now think, what product manufacturer would produce a product and never ask its audience what they think of it? Agile allows marketers to transition into a new world of building from data and executing via automation, and the review process is a critical component.

Some marketers make excuses to justify their lack of review. They say, "Customers don't want to talk to us," or they believe their customers will have their phone calls blocked. Sure, not everyone wants to talk to you, but many do and are happy to. To increase your odds of success, make sure you have a list of about twenty people you can call with a set of quick, easy, and specific questions. Personally, I find the best system for reviewing an effort is to ask three questions:

1. What brought you to that moment?

2. What were your expectations, and did we meet them?

3. Have other brands produced better experiences? Which ones?

I've found that calling twenty people and asking these questions will net you around six conversations, providing you with ample information to guide your iteration. The answers to these questions will give you the insights you need to refine your strategy, reach more people in context, and meet their desire in the moment. Once your program has been completed, much of it can run on its own. In time, you'll likely have hundreds of programs running across the entire customer life cycle, leaving you time to focus only on managing programs and introducing the refinements demanded by changing conditions. You'll begin now to manage your programs in an agile way, using data to focus you on the experiences needing your attention in the moment, driving the most value for your brand with your effort.

Using Agile Backlogs to Keep You Focused

Now that you're starting to see a new world where you build your customer-journey programs in iterative steps, and where your daily tasks shift to managing and optimizing hundreds of automated programs, there's one final aspect of agile that's critically important: producing the highest value per unit of time. Key to this is the backlog.

What makes agile so valuable is its ability to focus a team on the most important short-term goals for testing ideas and immediately incorporating insights. In other words, agile helps brands focus on and produce whatever experience has the highest value now. But since time is limited, that means a lot of good ideas won't take priority—and could easily get lost (and often do). That's why backlogs are a crucial element of the agile method.

Backlogs are living lists organized by the marketing team's collective view of an item's *business impact*. At the top of the list, the team places the make-or-break items for reaching business goals; at the bottom are nice-to-haves. To determine this "collective view" of where an idea or task belongs on the backlog, teams use open discussion coupled with a simple 100 Point exercise.

The 100 Point exercise asks team members to assign points to ideas and tasks that, in their view, have the biggest impact on business goals (not marketing goals, but goals for the business overall). Each team member gets 100 points to assign to the tasks on the backlog. Points are awarded based on how critical the item or task is believed to be by the team member. Whereas a believed business-stopping item may receive thirty points, a new blog post may receive only one point. Once everyone has deployed their points, the totals for each item are then added up and the priorities reordered, with the items winning the most points at the top. This ensures that the projects with the biggest impact on the business are completed first, with the others taken on in turn.

Backlogs also help your team manage its new workload, with its many moving parts. New requests are added to the backlog and prioritized by consensus; so instead of tackling items based on when they come in, they are completed only when the team rates them as the best use of resources. That way, the backlog gives each team member the leverage to say no when there's a better use of time, which leads to one of the biggest benefits of the agile process: the team's sanity. You not only have a powerful way to rank tasks based on business impact—not on who has the loudest voice—but you also have a way for team members to communicate their goals and achievements that the rest of the organization can understand.

The concept of the backlog also implies a new way for the marketing team to operate day to day. Rather than working on projects from whoever has the loudest voice, team members stay focused on producing the highest returns. Customer journeys are monitored and constantly optimized, and daily tasks are sorted based on potential impact.

I'll close this chapter with an answer I got to the question, What's the best part about agile? "The big win is in people looking at their work in a fundamentally new way," said one of my unnamed sources from the bank. "They are now very focused on how we add the most value with the least amount of effort." Capital One should know: the bank made a big bet and moved the operations of its entire marketing team to the agile method and hasn't looked back.

That focus on value is an important part of making the case for context marketing. As the role of marketing takes on a bigger piece of the business, it is imperative that we seek not only new marketing ideas and tools but also new ways of working in order to handle the expanded task load. Agile can sound like a complex answer to a complex problem, when in fact—like most brilliant ideas—it's actually a simplification, providing brands with more value for less effort.

What's more, embracing agile is how we move toward the final step of the context marketing revolution: becoming a contextual organization. The transition to a contextual organization requires more than just adopting the context framework. It requires a reconfiguring of the business model and marketing's role in it, new executive leadership, and a new way of reporting on marketing's value. These changes are not small, which is why understanding how to test and prove results via the agile method is critical. Now that you have a solid understanding of why we need context and how to execute it, let's take the final step and look at how high-performing marketing organizations realign their businesses around a new idea of marketing—the context marketing model—and complete their transition into becoming modern brands.

13.

A New Business Model for the Context Marketing Revolution

Build, market, sell. That's been standard procedure ever since the Industrial Revolution—a business model that confines marketing's role to introducing the product, a mere intermediary between production and sales. The model is quintessential limited media era, but one that practically everyone continues to follow—to their detriment.

Consider Mercedes-Benz. The ninety-year-old company, known as one of the world's top luxury brands, uses an operating model of *build-market-sell* and focuses heavily on its grand advertising campaigns. By contrast, Tesla, a company that's only thirteen years old, has outsold Mercedes to become the number-one luxury car in 2018. Indeed, Tesla is the poster child of the context marketing revolution. Its business model is born of the infinite media era: marketing is intrinsic to every aspect of the business—from the location of showrooms, to the booking of test drives, to the purchase of vehicles, to the amassing of thousands of advocates who help fund the next Tesla vehicle design in progress. Tesla's business model of *market-sell-build-market* is what I consider the consummate context marketing model (CMM).

We'll begin this chapter with a further exploration of Tesla's methods compared with Mercedes-Benz. Then I'll describe a new C-suite role that brands will need if they hope to execute experiences seamlessly and adopt this new idea of marketing. From there we'll look at how to value your contextual marketing efforts, how to continue those efforts postpurchase, and how to gain buy-in for context marketing across organizational teams.

Tesla: Context Marketing Throughout the Journey

When you compare Mercedes-Benz and Tesla, the market-first model wins hands-down. Where Mercedes focuses on mass advertising as its growth model, Tesla doubles down on context across the entire customer journey to fuel its growth.

Marketing at Tesla begins in the *ideation* stage of the customer journey, with the company's well-known focus on a shared purpose: getting the world off fossil fuels. This focus on sustainable living through radical innovation—rather than focusing on electric cars only—is the heart of Tesla's brand strategy. Most articles written about Tesla showcase its unusual business strategy and unconventional choices, such as launching a car into outer space. (It helps when the company founder also owns a space exploration enterprise.) Mercedes-Benz, on the other hand, is only about the cars. This key difference explains why, as of 2018, Tesla has been mentioned more than twenty-three thousand times on CNN.com, compared with five thousand mentions on the same channel for Mercedes-Benz. And even though much of the press Tesla garners is on topics other than electric cars, its powerful purpose-focus spills over to the product conversation. Tesla's current market share of the electric car conversation is the largest, at 22 percent, while Mercedes-Benz is eighth at 5 percent.[1]

In addition to ideation, Tesla has also mastered context at other stages of the customer journey. In the *consideration* stage, it dominates the results of every major search term related to electric cars. A recent search for "best electric car" turns up a *U.S. News & World Report* article on the eight best electric cars: two of them are Teslas, with the Model 3 getting an honorable mention.[2] No other electric car manufacturer is mentioned more than once in the report.

In the *purchase* stage, Tesla has replaced the dreaded, time-consuming process of negotiating with a salesperson with an experience that Paula

Tompkins, writing for ChannelNet, an omnichannel marketing site, describes as "empowering": she simply used the website to schedule her own test drive and within seconds received a text confirming her appointment. Shortly afterward, she received an email with a link to MyTesla.com, a personalized site where she could configure her own car and go deep into the details she cared about, on her own time. Tompkins was also paired with an owner advisor (not a salesperson), who helped Tompkins weigh options and further develop her understanding of the car. That conversation directly affected her choice in the end, helping her decide that the all-wheel-drive option was not for her.[3]

Tesla's contextual effectiveness in the *customer* stage may be the most impressive of all. The company provides 24/7 tech support and proactively alerts owners when maintenance is due. After a bit of time, Tesla transitions owners into advocates by introducing them to its referral programs, which offer a cash incentive of $1,000 to both the Tesla owner and the friend who purchases a car based on the referral. *PC Magazine* reported that a top advocate, known by his handle Wei70644, referred a whopping 188 people who also purchased a car, singlehandedly bringing in $16 million in sales for Tesla, at a cost of around $135,000 for his prizes.[4] That's a strong driver of revenue, and all of these stages taken together is what a connected, contextual brand experience looks like from start to finish.

Comparing Mercedes's *build-market-sell* model with the CMM used by Tesla (*market-sell-build-market*) is revealing. When Tesla began taking orders for its midpriced Model 3 in May 2016, more than two hundred thousand customers had paid deposits to reserve one in the first twenty-four hours (before the physical product even existed), and Tesla raked in over $10 billion in presales globally. Domestically it presold 270,000 units, three times the total sales of all (not just electric) domestic Mercedes-Benz C Class cars *in the same year*. What's more, Tesla pulled off this hugely successful launch without a grand campaign or so much as a tagline. An impressive feat, no doubt, yet even more impressive is that the average cost of advertising per car for the Model 3 was $6,[5] compared with Mercedes's $926.

Tesla is just one example of how the infinite era is forcing businesses to adopt an operational model that realigns the business around creating contextual experiences, but it proves the power of doing so. It had no need to advertise, because contextual marketing was inherently part of the way Tesla ran its business: meeting people where they are and only when they're already interested in spending time and connecting through a higher purpose.

You might be thinking, well of course Tesla succeeded—it was built during the infinite era, from the ground up. So, what if your company has been entrenched in limited era practices for decades, if not nearly a century as Mercedes has been? How can any business make such a transition without throwing itself into chaos? As I've tried to make clear throughout this book, not only is such a change possible, but it's also necessary for survival. Having a chief experience officer on board will help make it happen.

The CXO: Leading Customer Experience Across the Business

Context-based marketing requires a new executive whose operational bounds extend far past traditional marketing and deep into all departments. That person is the chief experience officer (CXO), whose primary task will be to ensure that the context of the customer—that moment-to-moment experience—drives every action your company takes in each stage of the journey.

This role isn't a new idea, as it was first proposed in *The Experience Economy* back in 1999, but now it is gaining serious traction in the market. Contextual brands around the world are shifting toward this role—acknowledging that marketing is a primary economic driver of the business and putting a CXO at the executive table. In 2017, Publicis, the oldest and one of the world's largest marketing agencies, hired a CXO, and in 2018, J.Crew hired longtime Starbucks executive Adam Brotman as CXO, placing him second-in-command to CEO Jim Brett. The list of similar appointments across industries is growing, along with a notable evolution in the roles and responsibilities in the C-suite.

For many brands this transition may already be in play. At Motorola, for example, Eduardo Conrado moved from his position as chief marketing officer to become senior VP of marketing and IT in 2013. As Conrado told *Ad Age:* "Our view is that, more and more, technology is a business enabler. . . . And as more companies are centered on the customer, then IT should also be supercharging the customer engagements of the company. . . . The CMO has been knee-deep in technology strategy. It's a natural fit."[6] In 2015 Motorola went further to include customer experience under Conrado's command, expanding his purview. While Conrado's title isn't CXO, rather EVP–Chief Strategy and Innovation Office, he describes his role as "responsible for managing the company's growth-focused strategy, accelerating innovation across the company's products, services and software, and bringing a design-centric approach to business model and customer experience innovation" on his LinkedIn profile.

The CXO, or whatever title you choose, must be the owner of all contextual efforts, including the technology—the contextual platform—and must ensure that all leaders are actively contributing to the customer journey strategy. The person in this role can be nothing less than a master of collaboration, with a central focus on experiences. The technology linked in the contextual platform won't work without teams across the business acting more interdependently than ever before. And that kind of collaboration requires strong modeling in the C-suite. In fact, according to the Salesforce study, high-performing marketing organizations are seventeen times better at collaborating across the entire customer life cycle than underperformers.[7]

As your organizational structure changes, previous titles take on a new function under the CXO. The CMO transitions to a more creative role responsible for the brand voice, acting more like a traditional art director or creative director. The CIO transitions from managing internal networks to managing the hosted network of systems used to obtain and share the data that drives the contextual platform. The CXO and the CIO work closely together to ensure the technologies that support brand experiences evolve as quickly as possible and in line with government regulations. As Ingrid Purcell, CXO of ME Bank in Australia, describes it, her role is "the perfect blend of creativity, customer focus, and technology."[8]

With a new executive able to build bridges across all departments focused on creating a contextual customer experience, brands must take the next step: proving these efforts are worthwhile.

Context Marketing Efforts: What Are They Worth?

Marketing departments have long struggled with proving the value of their efforts. The distance between a brand experience and final outcomes leaves any metric proving value subjective at best. Such lack of objective measures has held marketers back from achieving greater status in organizations worldwide. It's also no doubt contributed to the short tenure of marketing leaders.

When the data science team at LinkedIn and I looked at fifteen million data points to investigate employment life cycles, we made a shocking discovery. The average tenure of a marketing professional across all business verticals was the shortest of any role in the business world: just 2.6 years. That's less than the lifespan of a hamster! Fortunately, along with everything else that has changed in the infinite media era, so has the way marketing can prove its ever-growing value to any organization. It starts with a new way to showcase marketing's value.

Businesses everywhere have the idea that return on investment (ROI) proves the value and effectiveness of anything, be it a channel, tactic, or action. But that measurement is the wrong one to value marketing. Dominique Hanssens, former director of the Marketing Science Institute and Distinguished Research Professor at UCLA's Anderson School of Management, focuses on this question: What is the short- and long-run impact of marketing on business performance? Hanssens and I have discussed this topic at great length, and we firmly believe ROI and attribution methodologies are insufficient valuation methods for marketing activities.

First, capital expenditures and percentage returns are based on annualized time frames. Marketing results, however, are not annualized or even finite in their returns. Investment in marketing activities today may not see returns for some time, but that doesn't mean the investments were unwise or that they didn't produce the highest value for the company. They simply do not track to an annual measurement.

Second, in many cases, marketing returns are not financial. So using a financial metric to measure a result not tied to a financial outcome is ill matched. Take the ROI of an email. There is virtually no cost to creating or sending an email. Many times, the email engagement is many steps removed from the actual purchase, yet we use ROI to show the value of that effort.

Hanssens likes to point out another major flaw with ROI: it is not a linear return. If you get a 25 percent ROI on the first $100 invested, you won't see the same results on the second investment. So a 25 percent ROI on the first $100 does not guarantee a 25 percent return on the second investment. It may actually take $110 or $200 to obtain the same 25 percent ROI. So if ROI is used as an investing guide, it can lead to underinvestment in marketing programs.

On top of everything else, ROI is a numerical representation of what we've done in the past, but it provides no guidance on how to improve future outcomes. And yet, despite all of these ways that ROI is problematic for showing marketing's value, it remains the number-one method that businesses use to value our efforts.

A more advanced—but still flawed—way to use ROI is emerging in attribution and influence reporting, which suggests that ROI shouldn't be tied to all marketing "touches"—or actions—but rather only to those actions that influence consumers' decisions. Or, in terms of attribution, actions that have the highest influence on consumers' decisions. According to this ROI theory, attribution and influence can be calculated in one of three ways:

1. **First touch attribution** gives the credit to the first marketing campaign to find the lead as the most influential marketing touch, receiving the most credit.

2. **Equal attribution** equally spreads the revenue across all campaigns that touched the person.

3. **Last touch attribution** ascribes value only to the last marketing campaign a person interacted with before converting into a customer.

The assumptions behind each of these calculations are more advanced than basic ROI. However, they are still flawed for two key reasons: they do not take into account the full experience, and they still do not show any real value, because they are still assuming ROI is a value metric. To give you some clear examples of how flawed these reporting methods are, I spent some time talking with Gary Angel, former head of digital analytics for

Ernst and Young, and we came up with the following examples to help you better see the flawed logic of these supposedly improved valuations.

Statement: Our traffic is up!

- **Valuation Type #1 First Touch Attribution:** Searches for our company name are up, so our brand is improving.

- **Valuation Type #2 Equal Attribution:** Our investment in SEO is having a positive ROI.

- **Valuation Type #3 Last Touch Attribution:** That last advertisement was amazing! Do more advertising!

- **More Probable Explanation:** We have more visitors with customer support issues because our last release was awful. (When you use ROI to value marketing efforts without seeing the full picture, often it will lead you to the wrong conclusions.)

Note that the first action had nothing to do with the increase in traffic, even though it was the first touch the business took to engage the customer. Equal attribution believes everything is benefiting the result, while last touch focuses on the effect of the last campaign on the increased traffic and assigns a correlation—but there isn't one. The larger trend is not seen by the ROI calculations, so relying on ROI only leads to decisions based on poor assumptions. Let's look at another.

Statement: Our online revenue is up!

- **Valuation Type #1 First Touch Attribution:** A direct mail flyer from two years ago is paying huge dividends now.

- **Valuation Type #2 Equal Attribution:** All of our marketing is amazing, keep it up!

- **Valuation Type #3 Last Touch Attribution:** The ROI on the last email is killer. Send more emails!

- **More Probable Explanation:** Offline customers are shifting online, but they spend less money with us than they used to.

Once again, the first action had nothing to do with the outcome, even though it was the first engagement. Equal attribution believes everything is benefiting the result, while last touch suggests there's a correlation with email—and there isn't one. The larger trend is not seen by these calculations, so relying on attribution or any variation of ROI leads to decisions based on poor assumptions.

With the shift in the infinite media era to using strategies focused on the customer journey, marketers must expand their idea of value past how well a campaign performed. They need to show a clear picture of the health of the entire customer journey, as well as *how quickly and efficiently* individuals are moving across it. With marketing now the owners of every brand experience, we need to track the experience from start to finish and show how we've affected it. Most important, we need to prove how our efforts affect total revenue.

The only way to see a full picture of the customer experience in a single view—and track context marketing's impact on it—is to use a new reporting method: the weighted pipeline model. That will mean giving up old ideas of ROI and embracing this new holistic and predictive measure. By seeing the entire customer journey in a single model, marketers can showcase many value metrics, such as (1) net new demand, (2) future demand, (3) how marketing affects customers' motivation across the journey, (4) increases in existing revenue through decreasing customer churn, and (5) increased brand advocacy.

More and more, businesses will be giving marketing an elevated place in the C-suite and making it a primary business driver. We therefore must be able to value our work in a way that can be tracked and reported on a balance sheet, which is what the weighted pipeline is. ROI can't do that.

Using the Weighted Pipeline Model to Measure Value

The executive leadership in your company doesn't care whether email open rates have increased; they want to know the effect of those achievements on business outcomes. The weighted pipeline is the reporting model that can measure the full value of marketing's success in bringing in new business and retaining current customers. It is holistic, objective, and an accepted method already used in many businesses, mainly in the sales department. (Venture capital firms also use it to determine business valuations, and publicly traded companies use it to report future growth on reporting calls to investors.) Now that your context marketing approach is run on an automated platform with the ability to track all touch points across all of the customer journeys associated with a brand, you'll be able to use the weighted pipeline valuation model and show marketing's true value.

Here's how it works: the weighted pipeline model examines each member of your brand audience and the likelihood for each to convert into revenue, even how much revenue, at a future point in time. It makes these determinations using historical business data combined with the real-time personal data gathered by your contextual platform, and therefore is highly accurate. It's also holistic: it takes into account all actions, even unknown factors outside our control, such as word of mouth. After all, it isn't a single experience that drives a person to purchase; rather, it's a large combination and variety of experiences. By looking at how the experiences, taken together, move individuals through the various stages, you can see how all your efforts are working together. But the weighted pipeline also takes into account the effects of your efforts that you can't necessarily see, because you are not looking at individual actions but net outcomes. Weighted pipeline results are also prescriptive: they show you where your journeys are breaking down, so you can fix them and prove that the prescriptive action actually worked.

Let's take a look at the weighted pipeline model translated into contextual marketing terms by examining its four parts: volume, velocity, efficiency, and probability.

1. **Volume.** Volume is the number of people in a given stage of the customer journey at any particular point in time. You will have total volume, as well as the volume of each stage. To measure volume you need a container. Depending on how your tools connect, this may be a marketing tool or your customer relationship management (CRM) tool.

Each stage of the journey should be defined as the period of time in which a specific set of questions/actions is happening. In a B2C environment, stages may be categorized by buyer type or persona, such as first-time buyer, repeat buyer, advocate, and so on. All of these segments give us a solid understanding of the average total order size and an average length of the full buying cycle.

2. **Velocity.** Velocity is the measure of how quickly leads are moving through the customer journey. Again, you have velocity per stage, and as a whole. Velocity answers the question, Is the full customer experience moving this person in a positive direction, and if so, how quickly? If we know that the period from first ideation touch point to closed business takes a certain amount of time—let's say forty-five days—this can be used to accurately predict future outcomes. It can also show a new value of marketing: decreasing the sales cycle. For example, if in the future marketing looks at the report and sees average time to complete a journey is now thirty days, marketing can show that it decreased the sales cycle by 33 percent. If marketing's contextual efforts can speed that journey, it creates more sales cycles per year—a value that marketing can now measure.

3. **Efficiency.** The weighted pipeline measures not only how fast people are moving from stage to stage but also how *efficiently* they are moving through the pipeline. If you have a pipeline with only three stages, and you increase the efficiency of each stage by 1 percent, you then increase the total outcome by 28 percent. This means you would increase total revenue by 28 percent, simply by increasing the efficiency of each stage by 1 percent. It should also be noted that the increase is not a spike, quickly returning to its former low as you would see with a traditional marketing campaign. Rather, it is a sustained increase lasting well into the future.

4. **Probability.** This measures the likeliness that your prospective customer will turn into revenue. Both efficiency and probability measure the effectiveness of your demand model, but in two different

ways. Efficiency between stages is a powerful way for you to show the value of specific programs or efforts, while probability looks at the connection to the larger journey in terms of revenue—the number your executives care about. When marketing can measure the speed of each stage in the customer journey *and* the average probability of becoming a customer, revenue outcomes become *very* predictable. ROI can't do that.

How to Create a Weighted Pipeline Model and Reports

The weighted pipeline model acts as a balance sheet, providing a snapshot of the current health of the customer journey. This view offers insight into changes to the revenue stream. Table 13-1 provides a simple example of a calculated weighted pipeline for all stages of a customer journey. You can see the total number of people in each stage (volume); the average time people stay within each stage; how quickly they move through the stage; how efficiently your efforts move those people from stage to stage; and the probability of someone at any stage becoming a customer.

The revenue metric is pulled from your sales team, and in this example the average order size is $10,000. Note that when calculating the weighted

TABLE 13-1

Measuring total demand with the weighted pipeline

Stage	Volume	Velocity	Efficiency	Probability	Weighted value
Ideation	100	5 days	70%	10%	$(100 \times .1) \times \$10,000$
Awareness	70	9 days	77%	14%	$(70 \times .14) \times \$10,000$
Consideration	54	10 days	40%	20%	$(54 \times .2) \times \$10,000$
Purchase	21	30 days	50%	50%	$(21 \times .5) \times \$10,000$
Net new pipeline total	290	54 days	**Net new pipeline value**		**$411,000**
Customer	200	75	10%	10%	$(200 \times .10) \times \$20,000$
Advocate pipeline total					**$400,000**

pipeline as a person progresses in the journey from the *customer* stage to becoming an *advocate*, you need to take into account the increased average purchase size of advocates. In the example below, I've used $20,000. Also note the weighted pipeline ends at the *customer* stage. That's because lifetime customer value (LCV) is the better measure for marketing's impact on advocacy (see the next section).

Just as a balance sheet opens doors to new metrics—like debt-to-equity ratio, inventory turnover, and average age of receivables—the weighted pipeline model is the foundation for many new marketing reports. Marketing can show total future demand in a single revenue number by adding together the (volume × probability) of each stage, as noted by $411,000 in table 13-1. This "pipeline total" metric allows marketing to translate its full efforts directly into a single revenue number. Tracking changes with this number easily translates marketing efforts into actual business value.

The model also tracks the total time it takes to complete the journey, which allows marketing to track and show its effect on customer motivation and to track the customer journey as a whole. Finally, new reports such as velocity by stage and efficiency by stage can be used to show the value of granular efforts while highlighting specific issues within the journey.

With new reports possible using the weighted pipeline model, it will be up to you and your executive team to choose which reports you share at board meetings. Now that marketing is a string of connected experiences, however, our reporting must be able to show their combined effect and translate those efforts into a number that our executives respect—revenue. The weighted pipeline model offers the best way to show marketing's holistic value.

Postpurchase Marketing Efforts: The LCV Reward

While the weighted pipeline model measures current demand at each stage in the customer journey, LCV measures how your efforts *are generating more revenue* by extending the contract time and size of each deal. When tracking LCV, you need to focus on three things: tenure, churn rate, and

TABLE 13-2

Weighted pipeline for measuring LCV

Stage	Tenure	Churn	Weighted LCV
Customer	455 days	5%	$(\$10{,}000 \times (455/365)) \times (1 - .05)$
LCV of a customer			**$11,842.00**
Advocate	1,200 days	2%	$(\$20{,}000 \times (1{,}200/365)) \times (1 - .02)$
LCV of an advocate			**$64,438.00**

average order size. In the customer stage, tenure marks how long a customer or an advocate stays a paying client, while churn is the average percentage of customers who leave each year. You'll need to use an updated annualized contract value for your advocates, since they typically spend much more than regular customers do. As I did in the previous table, here I've used $20,000 for advocate spending (see table 13-2).

LCV calculations allow you to report on the average value of each customer—and how you arrived at that increased value. Are they simply spending more money, staying longer, or are you able to keep more of them as customers? This model will answer those questions for you, while showing how well you're using marketing methods to gain more profit from customers and advocates.

Apart from providing a superior metric, the weighted pipeline model also becomes a guide. When marketing uses a weighted pipeline, each number in the model becomes a signal, alerting the team of issues in the journey, where to focus, and which actions will result in the best use of marketers' time. By combining agile methods with weighted pipeline reporting, brands now can know where to focus, which ensures they are delivering the highest value to the businesses per unit of time.

As powerful as reporting is, you'll have to take one more step to make the full transition to context marketing: getting the buy-in of other departments. Many of the programs contextual marketers create are far outside marketing's traditional scope. Onboarding programs affect the product team, new sales nurturing programs affect the sales process, and automated support follow-ups affect the service team. Each team and department must be brought into the process to ensure its success. Rather than doing that in a forceful way, read on to learn how to secure a smooth transition to a co-operative approach throughout your organization.

Gaining Buy-in for Contextual Marketing Across Teams

Now that marketing is owning the customer experience across all touch points, there are many new teams—from sales to production—that you must work with. Building brand experiences together that those other teams will have faith in—and will support—is just as critical to your success as anything else. Once you gain the trust of those teams and involve them in the process, outcomes dramatically improve.

Of all the teams you'll work with, sales is typically the most challenging. But if you learn to build better experiences *with* them, not just *for* them, you'll gain a solid foundation that you can replicate with other teams and departments.

Gaining the trust of sales begins with recognizing that those folks know many specifics about how your customer makes a purchase that you likely don't. Sales is a highly skilled position, and teams are typically an assertive bunch. Your best salespeople get results because they are smart. Sales is a repeatable process, and your best reps have already built a great process. Your programs should follow that process. If you try to come in and reinvent the wheel, your efforts will get stymied at arguably the most important stage of the customer journey: purchase.

So single out your best salesperson, maybe two, and book time with them to ask about their process. Understand how they identify objections, what emails they send, and when. Most great salespeople have several versions of their emails, and they constantly refine them with phrases that are landing well. They also likely have them all saved in a document for easy copying and pasting. Get your hands on those emails! This will be your email content. Try to use them "as is" to the extent possible. It doesn't matter if they're not pretty. What matters is that sales has confidence in them. The key here—at least at first—is to mimic what those salespeople do. Not only will that help you do a better job, but it will also gain their trust and bring them on as partners in your effort.

Next, find out the most common objections they face from customers and potential customers. Those objections will inform which automated programs you build first to help trigger customers to take the next step forward along their journey. Build programs only for *common* objections, such as the following:

- I'm not ready to buy; call me in sixty days.

- I've not had time to go over any of this yet.

- I'm already using a competitive solution.

Next, ask salespeople how they handle such objections. Their answers will be a golden input to your strategy because great salespeople usually follow some type of timed process. When I was selling, we called this a *cadence*. My cadence was 2-2-12. I would call and leave a voicemail upon getting a new lead. Then I would wait two days and call back, but leave no voicemail and send no email. I'd then call again in two more days and leave another voicemail and send an email. Then I'd wait twelve days and do it all over again. These cadences will become the strategy that guides the timing of your automated program.

By mimicking the best salespeople, you'll also get the rest of the sales team to buy into your context marketing program. If you skip this legwork, your sales team simply won't cooperate, and your contextual efforts will never get off the ground.

Use this same process with every program that requires buy-in from other teams across the organization: your support team, your client services management team, and your product team all have lots of intelligence that you'll need to incorporate as, together, you create and manage your river of amazing brand experiences. Ask those teams, involve them, learn to work with them. They have a lot of specific knowledge that will be critical to your success. By working together, you will all succeed.

The changes required to become a contextual marketing organization are not simple, or small. It requires new executive team members, a new method of working, a new business model, and even a new way of reporting. This is a significant amount of change for the entire organization, not just marketing. To drive this change, your chief executive must be on board. Remember, the number-one trait of high-performing marketing organizations is *they have full executive buy-in to a new idea of marketing.* You now know what context marketing entails and how to execute it. In the next, concluding chapter, let's cover your first step to making the needed changes, and where you must begin: gaining executive buy-in.

14.

The First Step, and Final Thoughts

Context marketing as I've outlined it in this book is the future of marketing, brands, and your business. But these aren't simple iterations. The reality is that making any of the changes we've explored here will take time and a significant amount of work. Most of all, they'll require the full support of and buy-in from the executive team, which brings us to the very first step you will need to take: proving to your top executives that contextual marketing is the correct path forward.

Gaining Executive Buy-in

Change isn't easy, and getting your executive team to give up old methods of driving demand to embrace a radically new one is no small task. Executives are often the hardest to persuade of anyone in the organization. What will it take to change their minds, especially when your new idea will shift the structure of the business? I've seen only two ways to persuade a top executive to embrace ideas that require significant change: (1) a paid consultant or esteemed colleague (outside the firm) made the case for change, or (2) the executive team was persuaded by internal testing.

Consultants are a gamble. There are way too many of them, and very few are excellent. So do your homework if you take that road. In 2013, the

Atlantic Monthly reported that there were 181,345 social media experts available for hire (and surely many, many more today).[1] I did my own investigation of that list, and far too many had no formal education or practical expertise of any kind. And from what I could determine from their LinkedIn profiles, even those with practical expertise tend to hold onto their beliefs rather than changing them over time. If they do change, it's typically just an iteration; rarely do consultants give up their lifeblood in exchange for something fresh. It's too risky to their business. So be careful.

Another way to gain buy-in is for someone in your CEO's inner circle to make the case for you. But it's unlikely you'll have access to those people. You will, however, have this book. And I have found that many CEOs are voracious readers who can be persuaded by a strong, well-structured argument in a book. That's one of the main reasons I wrote this book—to help provide that "outside voice" that might make your case for these seemingly radical ideas.

But perhaps more convincing still, your team could experiment with a contextual effort using agile processes to create a minimum viable experience (MVE), as described in chapter 12's discussion of the agile process. Start small, iterate, and when you achieve success, present it to your CEO—along with this book. Backing up your case with internal data is always going to get more attention from leaders at the highest level.

Part of getting executive buy-in also means making a case for the budget you'll need to execute contextual marketing programs. The Salesforce 2016 *State of Marketing* research found that high-performing marketing organizations are increasing their marketing budgets in every category. The lowest rate of increase across traditional marketing spend, digital marketing spend, marketing consulting, marketing technology, and marketing headcount was 39 percent and went as high as 70 percent.[2] At the lowest level of investment, a budget growing at 39 percent per year *will double in 1.8 years.*

Of course, a significant increase in funding isn't likely to happen all at once. Usually it happens incrementally, growing alongside proven results. To accelerate that growth, you can adopt what I call a stretch budget.

The Stretch Budget

The idea of a stretch budget is simple: when you have an idea that you need to prove out, there should be a small fund you can access to create a case study. The trick to getting this budget is twofold. First, the conversation must happen before you need the money; and second, there must be defined rules for accessing the funds. Let's look at each of these qualifying characteristics.

First, the funding conversation with your boss has to happen before you need the money, because your stretch budget will operate much like a line of credit from a bank. It is negotiated beforehand, set aside, and accessed only when a specific set of criteria has been met.

When having the conversation about creating a stretch budget, couch it as an investment. If you can prove the effort you wish to undertake has a high and definable value, the company can then invest more at the right time. In setting up the terms of the deal, you must define the value on which success will be determined. Value can be measured in lots of ways, such as increased lead generation, registration numbers, total engagement, or pipeline improvement. The stretch is the delta by which you must improve the selected value metric.

For example, if your value is webinar registrations and your stretch number is 50 percent, you would have to drive a 50 percent increase in webinar attendance *over your current goal*. So if your goal was 300 registrants but you hit 450, you've just opened up an additional stretch budget to build out the contextual approach you leveraged to reach your stretch goal.

Second, have in mind the criteria for accessing the stretch budget so you can present that to your boss along with the preliminary funding proposition. Together you'll define the final criteria (or perhaps just your boss will), but bring to your meeting a possible answer to this question: How much of the total budget will be accessible at one time? A predetermined portion—instead of the whole amount after your first success—does a better job of getting leadership and other partners across the business to buy into the idea of testing and allocating budget for it. Once your idea has proven successful, then double down on those methods. Taking only a portion also allows for the stretch budget to be accessed multiple times.

With funds in place, you'll be able to test out your new ideas for creating contextual brand experiences and prove their value one at a time. That will grow your budget from your current starting point to where it needs to be, proving your methods to executive leadership and any skeptics every step of the way.

Final Thoughts on the Context Marketing Revolution

To review: gaining executive buy-in to engage with contextual marketing processes is paramount. Without it, you'll have neither the internal support to move past your historical scope nor the budget to execute a continuous flow of experiences. What's more, you'll be held back by old methods of reporting. To be sure, context marketing is not a small shift for businesses to make. But it's nonnegotiable for the survival of brands today. The proof is all around us, with brands of all shapes and sizes, spanning all corners of the globe, already embracing the kinds of contextual customer experiences that make marketing in the infinite media era tick.

But what if you can't get your executive team on board? This is a real possibility and one I'd like to address with you, the reader, on this very personal note: You have a career to consider, and you must keep in mind your future and your current employer's role in it. If you are unable to persuade your executives, team, or brand to move forward, consider whether you're in a company that's going to grow with the market—or fall irrevocably behind. Remember, not all brands survive. A brand that doesn't want to change is a brand in decline, and tying yourself to a sinking ship does you no good. Seek out companies that are willing to embrace change.

Meanwhile, think about this: every so often, a time in history emerges when radical change upends everything, and we look back at these periods as the "wild west" or the "golden days." As marketers, we look back to the time when branding and mass advertising swept through the world and created the rise of the adman (and fifty years later came the TV series to document it). Such magical periods of time are often hard to discern while we're in their midst. But make no mistake: we are in one of those periods now.

Perhaps such radical times are hard to identify because we continue trying to explain the changes through our preexisting ideas. Today our continued limited media era thinking leads us to focus on Tesla's Elon Musk—or the technology and design of Tesla cars—without giving credit to the company's deep, intrinsic understanding of context and its impeccable marketing execution as a primary driver of the business. Tesla's success and that of Airbnb and so many other breakout brands is often credited to the creative idea of the product. Yes, those ideas are radical and their products revolutionary, but an idea without proper execution fails.

Context marketing is how those brands grew, how they got their ideas to take hold. Calling it a revolution is not hyperbole. It is radical because it's what our time demands, and revolutionary because it is operating on a new foundation. Context is the new idea of marketing that brands must embrace—or suffer a slow but sure decline. Grim words, but on the other hand it's exciting to think about the impact our work can now have. In every industry, for-profit and nonprofits alike—education, consumer goods, healthcare, financial services, automotive, software, big or small, you name it—the same story holds true: brands that understand the significance of the infinite media era and see the power of context are not just succeeding. They are dominating the global marketplace.

Context isn't a marketing trick. It certainly isn't the evolution of old ideas. It's a revolution, a fundamental resetting of how we think about and execute business, driven by the greatest force of all—media. Marshall McLuhan had it right fifty years ago: the medium is the message. And the message is loud and clear: context is the revolutionary power we must use to break through the infinite noise, to motivate the modern buyer, and to drive growth.

Notes

Introduction

1. Zack Bloom, "The History of Email," Cloudflare Blog, September 23, 2017, https://blog.cloudflare.com/the-history-of-email/.

2. Combined total number of businesses surveyed in the Salesforce *State of Marketing* report from years 2016, 2017, 2018, and 2019.

3. Our research took place over four years, 2014–2018. We used blind studies in which we asked companies dozens of questions about what marketing tools and tactics they used and how well they worked across departments in their organizations.

4. Lori Wizdo, Caroline Roberts, Jacob Milender, Alexander Bullock, and Kara Hatig, "L2RM Practitioners Realize Performance Gains, but Significant Headroom Remains," https://www.forrester.com/report/L2RM+Practitioners+Realize+Performance+Gains+But+Significant+Headroom+Remains/-/E-RES141033.

5. Megan Brenan, "Nurses Again Outpace Other Professions for Honesty, Ethics," Gallup, December 20, 2018, https://news.gallup.com/poll/245597/nurses-again-outpace-professions-honesty-ethics.aspx.

6. Claudia Assis, "Tesla: Model 3 'Had Biggest One-Week Launch of Any Product Ever,'" Marketwatch, April 7, 2016, https://www.marketwatch.com/story/tesla-picks-up-325000-reservations-for-model-3-2016-04-07.

7. Joey Capprella, "The Best Selling Luxury SUV of 2018," *Car and Driver*, January 4, 2019, https://www.caranddriver.com/news/g25741172/best-selling-luxury-cars-suv-2018/.

Chapter 1

1. Gordon Donnelly, "Google Ads Mobile Benchmarks for Your Industry," WordStream Blog, August 27, 2019, https://www.wordstream.com/blog/ws/2018/08/13/google-ads-mobile-benchmarks.

2. Larry Kim, "Google Kills Off Side Ads, What You Need to Know," WordStream Blog, July 19, 2018, https://www.wordstream.com/blog/ws/2016/02/22/google-kills-off-right-side-ads.

3. Salesforce, *State of Marketing*, 2016, 58, https://www.salesforce.com/blog/2016/03/state-of-marketing-2016.html. This report is a global survey of 3,975 marketing leaders, where high performers were identified as those most satisfied with the outcomes of their marketing investments. With the high-performer cohort identified, we then compared how they rated their business's overall performance against that of their direct competition. Seventy-one percent of high performers rate their overall business's performance

much stronger than that of their direct competition. Only 1 percent of those dissatisfied with their marketing performance said the same.

4. Zack Bloom, "History of Email," Cloudflare Blog, September 23, 2017, https://blog.cloudflare.com/the-history-of-email/.

5. "Internet of Things Forecast," Ericsson, accessed October 30, 2019, https://www.ericsson.com/en/mobility-report/internet-of-things-forecast.

6. "World Energy Outlook 2017," International Energy Agency, accessed October 30, 2019, https://www.iea.org/sdg/.

7. Jenalea Howell, "Number of Connected IoT Devices Will Surge to 125 Billion by 2030, IHS Markit Says," IHS Markit, October 24, 2017, https://technology.ihs.com/596542/number-of-connected-iot-devices-will-surge-to-125-billion-by-2030-ihs-markit-says.

8. Jessica Wohl, "CKE Launches New Carl's Jr. Ads from New Agency Havas," *Ad Age*, February 19, 2018, http://adage.com/article/cmo-strategy/cke-launches-carl-s-jr-ads-agency-havas/312419/.

9. Craig Chamberlain, "Research Suggests Sexual Appeals in Ads Don't Sell Brands, Products," University of Illinois, June 22, 2017, https://news.illinois.edu/view/6367/522402.

10. Mark Irvine, "Google Ads Benchmarks for Your Industry," WordStream Blog, August 27, 2019, https://www.wordstream.com/blog/ws/2016/02/29/google-adwords-industry-benchmarks.

11. Elisa Shearer, "Social Media Outpaces Print Newspapers in the U.S. as a News Source," Pew Research Center, Fact Tank, December 10, 2018, https://www.pewresearch.org/fact-tank/2018/12/10/social-media-outpaces-print-newspapers-in-the-u-s-as-a-news-source/.

12. Josh Constine, "Zuckerberg Implies Facebook Is a Media Company, Just 'Not a Traditional Media Company,'" Techcrunch, December 21, 2016, https://techcrunch.com/2016/12/21/fbonc/.

13. Joseph Pine II and James H. Gilmore, *The Experience Economy: Work Is Theatre and Every Business a Stage* (Boston: Harvard Business School Press, 1999).

14. Aaron Pressman, "Why TaskRabbit's Gig Economy Model Is Thriving under Ikea's Ownership," *Fortune*, July 17, 2018, http://fortune.com/2018/07/17/taskrabbit-ikea-brown-philpot-undercover/.

15. Joseph Pine II and James H. Gilmore, "Welcome to the Experience Economy," *Harvard Business Review*, July–August 1998, https://hbr.org/1998/07/welcome-to-the-experience-economy.

16. Joseph Pine II and James H. Gilmore, *The Experience Economy*, updated ed. (Boston: Harvard Business Review Press, 2011).

17. Watermark Consulting, *2016 Customer Experience Study*, Insurance Industry ed., July 5, 2016, https://www.watermarkconsult.net/blog/2016/07/05/the-2016-customer-experience-roi-study-insurance-industry-edition/.

Chapter 2

1. Mark Prensky, "Digital Natives, Digital Immigrants," *On the Horizon* 9, no. 5 (October 2001), https://www.marcprensky.com/writing/Prensky%20-%20Digital%20Natives,%20Digital%20Immigrants%20-%20Part1.pdf.

2. Marshall McLuhan, *Understanding Media: The Extensions of Man* (Cambridge, MA: MIT Press, 1964).

3. Marshall McLuhan, *Understanding Me: Lectures and Interviews*, rev. ed. (Cambridge, MA: MIT Press, 2005).

4. Salesforce, *State of the Connected Customer*, 2019, https://www.salesforce.com /blog/2018/06/digital-customers-research.html.

5. Gary W. Small, Teena D. Moody, Prabba Siddarth, and Susan Y. Bookheimer, "Your Brain on Google: Patterns of Cerebral Activation during Internet Searching," *Psychology Today*, February 2009, https://www.psychologytoday.com/files/attachments /5230/136.pdf.

6. David S. White and Alison Le Cornu, "Visitors and Residents, New Typology for Online Engagement," *First Monday* 16, no. 9 (September 2011), http://firstmonday.org /ojs/index.php/fm/article/view/3171/3049.

7. Salesforce, *State of the Connected Customer*, 2017, https://www.salesforce.com /blog/2017/01/data-the-connected-customers-wants.html.

8. "AI Will Power 95% of Customer Interactions by 2025," *Finance Digest*, March 10, 2017, https://www.financedigest.com/ai-will-power-95-of-customer-interactions-by -2025.html.

9. Devon McGinnis, "Need-to-Know Marketing Statistics for 2019," Salesforce Blog, January 23, 2019, https://www.salesforce.com/blog/2019/01/marketing-statistics-to -know.html.

10. Julian Murphet, "Voice, Image, Television: Beckett's Divided Screens," SCAN, Macquarie University, Sydney, http://scan.net.au/scan/journal/display.php?journal _id=111.

11. "80% of Businesses Want Chatbots by 2020," Business Insider Intelligence, December 14, 2016, https://www.businessinsider.com/80-of-businesses-want-chatbots -by-2020-2016-12.

12. Kevin Mise, "Big AR: Android vs iOS," Hackernoon, July 31, 2017, https:// hackernoon.com/big-ar-android-vs-ios-3a683579eec8.

13. Salesforce, *State of the Connected Customer*, 2017.

14. Scott Huffman, "Here's How the Google Assistant Became More Helpful in 2018," Google Assistant Blog, January 7, 2019, https://www.blog.google/products /assistant/heres-how-google-assistant-became-more-helpful-2018/.

15. Kate Clark, "Here's Mary Meeker's 2019 Internet Trends Report," TechCrunch, June 11, 2019, https://techcrunch.com/2019/06/11/internet-trends-report-2019/.

16. "Ten Years on the Consumer Decision Journey: Where Are We Today?" McKinsey Blog, November 17, 2017, https://www.mckinsey.com/about-us/new-at-mckinsey -blog/ten-years-on-the-consumer-decision-journey-where-are-we-today.

17. Matt Lawson, "Win Every Micro-Moment with a Better Mobile Strategy," *Think With Google* Blog, September 2015, https://www.thinkwithgoogle.com/marketing -resources/micro-moments/win-every-micromoment-with-better-mobile-strategy/.

18. Zach Bulygo, "What the Highest Converting Websites Do Differently," KissMetrics Blog, accessed October 30, 2019, https://blog.kissmetrics.com/what-converting -websites-do/.

19. Emma Dunbar, "How Pinterest Drives Purchases Online and Off," Pinterest Blog, March 3, 2016, https://business.pinterest.com/en/blog/how-pinterest-drives -purchases-online-and-off.

20. David C. Edelman, "Branding in the Digital Age: You're Spending Your Money in All the Wrong Places," *Harvard Business Review*, December 2010, https://hbr.org /2010/12/branding-in-the-digital-age-youre-spending-your-money-in-all-the-wrong -places.

Chapter 4

1. "*Ad Age* Advertising Century: Top Ten Icons," *Ad Age*, March 29, 1999, https://adage.com/article/special-report-the-advertising-century/ad-age-advertising-century-top-10-icons/140157/.

2. Caitlin Dickson, "You Are More Likely to Survive an Airplane Crash Than You Are to Click a Banner Ad," *The Atlantic*, June 29, 2011, https://www.theatlantic.com/business/archive/2011/06/you-are-more-likely-survive-plane-crash-click-banner-ad/352323/.

3. "How Messaging Moves Business," Facebook IQ, 2019, https://www.facebook.com/iq/articles/more-than-a-message-messaging-means-business.

4. Elissa Hudson and Justin Lee, "Is Facebook Messenger the New Email? 3 Experiments to Find Out," HubSpot Blog, accessed October 30, 2019, https://blog.hubspot.com/marketing/facebook-messenger-marketing-experiments.

5. Mike Lewis, "Marketing Automation by the Numbers (infographic)," Business2Community, November 27, 2012, https://www.business2community.com/infographics/marketing-automation-by-the-numbers-infographic-0342287.

6. Salesforce, *State of Marketing*, 2018, https://www.salesforce.com/form/conf/5th-state-of-marketing/?leadcreated=true&redirect=true&chapter=&DriverCampaignId=70130000000sUVq&player=&FormCampaignId=7010M000000ZP24QAG&videoId=&playlistId=&mcloudHandlingInstructions=&landing_page=.

7. Stephen Pulvirent, "How Daniel Wellington Made a $200 Million Business out of Cheap Watches," Bloomberg, July 14, 2015, https://www.bloomberg.com/news/articles/2015-07-14/how-daniel-wellington-made-a-200-million-business-out-of-cheap-watches.

8. "Multiple Communities—and One Agency to Market Them All," Smartbug Media, accessed October 30, 2019, https://www.smartbugmedia.com/case-studies/arbor-company-success-with-gdd-cro-paid-inbound.

9. Maksym Gabielkov, Arthi Ramachandran, Augustin Chaintreau, and Arnaud Legout, "Social Clicks: What and Who Gets Read on Twitter?," Columbia University, April 13, 2016, https://hal.inria.fr/hal-01281190.

Chapter 5

1. Jeriad Zoghby, Scott Tieman, and Javier Pérez Moiño, *Making It Personal: Why Brands Must Move from Communication to Conversation for Greater Personalization*, Accenture Pulse Check, 2018, https://www.accenture.com/_acnmedia/pdf-77/accenture-pulse-survey.pdf.

2. Kara Sassone, "HubSpot Breaks World Record for Largest Webinar," HubSpot, updated July 4, 2013, https://www.hubspot.com/blog/bid/23564/HubSpot-Breaks-World-Record-For-Largest-Webinar.

3. Lindsey Finch, "Managing the Customer Trust Crisis: New Research Insights," Salesforce, September 6, 2018, https://www.salesforce.com/blog/2018/09/trends-customer-trust-research-transparency.html.

Chapter 6

1. "Beetle Overtakes Model T as World's Best-Selling Car," History, updated July 28, 2019, https://www.history.com/this-day-in-history/beetle-overtakes-model-t-as-worlds-best-selling-car.

2. Adam Blair, "Backcountry's Gearheads Leverage Expertise and Enthusiasm to Build Customer Relationships," *Retail TouchPoints*, November 15, 2015, https://www .retailtouchpoints.com/features/retail-success-stories/backcountry-s-gearheads-leverage -expertise-and-enthusiasm-to-build-customer-relationships.

3. Alen Bubich, "Is an Employee Advocacy Program More Powerful Than a Fan Page?," Social Horsepower, June 6, 2015, https://www.socialhp.com/blog/is-an-employee -advocacy-program-more-powerful-than-a-fan-page/.

4. Sander Biehn, "B2B Social Media Case Study: How I Made $47 Million from My B2B Blog," Business Grow Blog, accessed October 30, 2019, https://businessesgrow.com /2013/09/18/case-study-how-i-made-47-million-from-my-b2b-blog/.

Chapter 7

1. Elahe Izadi, "'Clearly We Missed the Mark': Pepsi Pulls Kendall Jenner Ad and Apologizes," *Washington Post*, April 5, 2017, https://www.washingtonpost.com/news /arts-and-entertainment/wp/2017/04/05/clearly-we-missed-the-mark-pepsi-pulls -kendall-jenner-ad-and-apologizes/.

2. Marisa Garcia, "Why Southwest Air Skips the Safety Videos in Favor of Free-Styling Flight Attendants," *Skift*, June 17, 2017, https://skift.com/2014/06/17/why -southwest-air-skips-the-safety-videos-in-favor-of-free-styling-flight-attendants/.

Chapter 8

1. Salesforce, *State of Marketing*, 2017, https://www.salesforce.com/content/dam /web/en_us/www/assets/pdf/datasheets/salesforce-research-fourth-annual-state-of -marketing.pdf.

2. Howard R. Bowen, *Social Responsibilities of the Businessman* (New York: Harper, 1953), 44.

3. R. W. Robins, K. H. Trzesniewski, J. L. Tracy, S. D. Gosling, and J. Potter, "Global Self-Esteem across the Life Span," *Psychology and Aging* 17, no. 3 (2002): 423–434, http://dx.doi.org/10.1037/0882-7974.17.3.423.

4. "Going #purplefortheplanet with Sambazon," Shorty Awards, 2018, https:// shortyawards.com/3rd-socialgood/going-purplefortheplanet-with-sambazon.

5. Gaurav Kheterpal, CTO, MTX Group, Salesforce Trailhead, accessed October 30, 2019, https://trailhead.salesforce.com/trailblazers/gaurav-kheterpal.

Chapter 9

1. The categories of doing, thinking, and feeling originated with the Adaptive Path Experience Mapping exercise published by Patrick Quattlebaum, "Download Our Guide to Experience Mapping," Adaptive Path, February 7, 2017, https://medium.com /capitalonedesign/download-our-guide-to-experience-mapping-624ae7dffb54. Adaptive Path was acquired by Capital One in 2015.

Chapter 10

1. Sapna Maheshwari, "Are You Ready for the Nanoinfluencers?," *New York Times*, November 11, 2018, https://nyti.ms/2DfqYyT.

2. Anum Hussain, "How to Launch and Grow a Business Blog from Scratch," HubSpot Blog, February 1, 2017, https://blog.hubspot.com/marketing/launch-grow -business-blog.

3. Eric Siu interviewing Mark Roberge, "GE 152: How HubSpot Skyrocketed from $0 to $200M by Combining Inbound Marketing + World Class Sales Training," in *Growth Everywhere*, podcast, accessed October 30, 2019, https://growtheverywhere.com /growth-everywhere-interview/mark-roberge-hubspot/.

4. Rebecca Corliss, "Why HubSpot Won't Exhibit at Trade Shows and Events Anymore," HubSpot Blog, February 1, 2017, https://blog.hubspot.com/blog/tabid /6307/bid/5461/Why-HubSpot-Won-t-Exhibit-at-Trade-Shows-and-Events -Anymore.aspx.

5. Salesforce, *State of Marketing*, 2016, https://www.salesforce.com/blog/2016/03 /state-of-marketing-2016.html.

6. Chris Anderson and Saram Han, *Hotel Performance Impact of Socially Engaging with Consumers*, Center for Hospitality Research, Cornell University, May 2016, https:// sha.cornell.edu/faculty-research/centers-institutes/chr/research-publications/hotel -performance-impact-socially-engaging-with-consumers.html.

7. Heike Young, *Shopper-First Retailing*, Salesforce, 2018, https://www.salesforce .com/blog/2018/08/digital-shopper-first-retail-report-research.

8. Frederick F. Reichheld and Phil Schefter, "E-Loyalty: Your Secret Weapon on the Web," *Harvard Business Review*, July–August 2000, https://hbr.org/2000/07/e-loyalty -your-secret-weapon-on-the-web.

9. Salesforce, *State of Marketing*, 2016.

Chapter 11

1. Salesforce, *State of Marketing*, 2018, https://www.salesforce.com/form/conf/5th -state-of-marketing/?leadcreated=true&redirect=true&chapter=&DriverCampaignId =70130000000sUVq&player=&FormCampaignId=7010M000000ZP24QAG&videoId =&playlistId=&mcloudHandlingInstructions=&landing_page=.

2. Salesforce, *State of Marketing*, 2017, https://www.salesforce.com/content/dam /web/en_us/www/assets/pdf/datasheets/salesforce-research-fourth-annual-state-of -marketing.pdf.

3. "Craveable Brands Drives Loyalty and $9 Million in Incremental Sales," case study, Salesforce, accessed November 5, 2019, https://www.salesforce.com/au/customer -success-stories/craveable/.

4. Heather Miller, "The Must-Knows of Reorganizing Sales and Marketing from Scratch with Associa's Matt Kraft," Salesforce for Sales, Medium, January 31, 2018, https://medium.com/salesforce-for-sales/the-must-knows-of-reorganizing-sales-and -marketing-from-scratch-with-associas-matt-kraft-eb585fdb03a9.

5. "Segment: How Drift Became Segment's #1 Source of Qualified Leads," case study, Drift, accessed November 5, 2019, https://www.drift.com/case-studies /segment/.

6. "LEGO: Increasing Sales Conversions with a Bot for Messenger," case study, Face-book Business, accessed November 5, 2019, https://www.facebook.com/business/success /2-lego.

7. LEGO Chatbot case study, Edelman Digital, accessed November 5, 2019, https:// edelmandigital.com/case-study/lego-chatbot/.

8. Morgan Brown, "Airbnb: The Growth Story You Didn't Know," GrowthHackers, Growth Studies, accessed November 5, 2019, https://growthhackers.com/growth-studies /airbnb.

Chapter 12

1. Sean Ellis, "Video: Agile Marketing Meetup—Satya Patel on Using the Scientific Method," GrowthHackers, 2015, https://growthhackers.com/videos/agile-marketing-meetup-satya-patel-on-using-the-scientific-method?comments=true.

2. Anthony Mersino, "Agile Project Success Rates 2X Higher Than Traditional Projects (2019)," Vitality Chicago, April 1, 2018, https://vitalitychicago.com/blog/agile-projects-are-more-successful-traditional-projects/.

3. Salesforce, *State of Marketing*, 2016, https://www.salesforce.com/blog/2016/03/state-of-marketing-2016.html.

4. "SAFe Case Study: Capital One," Scaled Agile, Inc., accessed October 30, 2019, https://www.scaledagileframework.com/capital-one-case-study/.

5. Andrea Fryrear, "Agile Marketing Examples & Case Studies," Agile Sherpas, accessed October 30, 2019, https://www.agilesherpas.com/agile-marketing-examples-case-studies/#Santander.

Chapter 13

1. Christophe Folschette, "Tesla's Marketing Strategy Shows That It's Time for CEOs to Get Social," TalkWalker Blog, July 25, 2019, https://www.talkwalker.com/blog/tesla-marketing-strategy-social-ceo.

2. John M. Vincent, "8 Best Electric Vehicles in 2018," *U.S. News & World Report*, July 30, 2018, https://cars.usnews.com/cars-trucks/best-electric-cars.

3. Paula Tompkins, "The Secrets behind Tesla's Awesome Customer Experience," Cross Channel Connection, March 21, 2016, https://crosschannelconnection.com/2016/03/21/secrets-behind-teslas-awesome-customer-experience/.

4. David Murphy, "Winner of Tesla Referral Promotion Hits 188 Orders," *PC Magazine*, January 2, 2016, https://www.pcmag.com/news/340797/winner-of-tesla-referral-promotion-hits-188-orders.

5. Steve Hanley, "Tesla Spends Just $6 per Car in Advertising," Teslarati, July 9, 2016, https://www.teslarati.com/tesla-spends-just-6-per-car-advertising/.

6. Abbey Klaassen, "Eduardo Conrado Talks about Motorola's Move to Marry Marketing—IT," *Ad Age*, May 8, 2013, https://adage.com/article/cmo-strategy/eduardo-conrado-talks-motorola-s-move-marry-marketing/241354.

7. Salesforce, *State of Marketing*, 2016, https://www.salesforce.com/blog/2016/03/state-of-marketing-2016.html.

8. Vanessa Mitchell, "CXO Profile: Customer Experience as the Key to Brand Survival," CMO.com, March 9, 2018, https://www.cmo.com.au/article/634405/cxo-profile-customer-experience-key-brand-survival/.

Chapter 14

1. J. K. Trotter, "181,354 People on Twitter Think They're Experts at Twitter," *The Atlantic*, January 7, 2013, https://www.theatlantic.com/technology/archive/2013/01/181354-people-twitter-think-theyre-experts-twitter/319793/.

2. Salesforce, *State of Marketing*, 2016, https://www.salesforce.com/blog/2016/03/state-of-marketing-2016.html.

Acknowledgments

No man is an island, and no book is the work of a single hand. I'd be re-miss if I didn't honor the numerous talented, dedicated, and brilliant indi-viduals who helped bring this book to life.

To the book development team, Annie Brunholzl and Lucy McCauley, I am truly grateful for your support, help, and most of all amazing work. You did more than I could have asked for. Thank you. To my agent, Esmond Harmsworth, thank you for all of your guidance, insight, and support. I honestly could not have done this without you.

To my executive editor, Jeff Kehoe, thank you for your foresight and unwavering support. It has meant the world to me. Thank you for the opportunity. I'll cherish it always.

To my boss, Bruce Richardson, I cannot thank you enough. Your coun-sel, support, and advocacy have been the underpinning of this entire ef-fort. Thank you for believing in me and helping bring this book to life. May your winters be mild, the Red Sox always above .500, and your evenings paired with the perfect red.

To the countless influences who have shaped my mind and feed my cu-riosities, I owe you more than these words can express. Jeff Rohrs, you have been a true friend, mentor, and sounding board. Thank you for open-ing up these doors for me and sending me down this path. Doc Searls, your writing sparked my imagination, and our conversations bolstered those ideas into what became this book. You are a brilliant and humble man, and I thank you for all that you have done.

Eric McLuhan and Andrew McLuhan, your father/grandfather was a special man, and his brilliance has illuminated much of my life and work. Thank you for your time, conversation, and willingness to share his legacy with me. Joe Pine, thank you for the numerous conversations, support, and feedback. They were invaluable.

To all of the numerous others who have supported this book and pushed me onward, I owe you my gratitude. This has been a dream come true. I could not have done it without you.

Thank you.

Index

About the Author

MATHEW SWEEZEY is Principal of Marketing Insights for Salesforce and is regarded as one of the leading minds on the future of marketing. His visionary insights into consumer behavior, technology, and new business strategies have changed the way startups, *Fortune* 500 brands, and nonprofit organizations alike find customers, break through, and build modern brands. Prior to his current role, Mathew was an early pioneer of the marketing automation space and played a key role in the success of the marketing automation technology company Pardot (now a part of the Salesforce Marketing Cloud).

As a futurist, Mathew has had the distinct privilege of working alongside Peter Schwartz, world-renowned futurist and author, *The Art of the Long View*. Through Schwartz, Mathew was introduced to his unique future-think and scenario-planning processes continuing the legacy of legendary futurists Pierre Wack and Herman Kahn. This unique vantage point guides much of Mathew's thinking, research, and work with brands.

As a researcher, Mathew has helped conduct numerous studies for leading organizations such as LinkedIn and The Economist Group to help brands better understand the modern consumer and his or her innermost desires. His research often focuses on the intersection of media, psychology, and technology.

In addition to his research, Mathew is a powerful speaker, a highly sought after keynote speaker at conferences across the globe, and the host of the award-winning podcast *The Electronic Propaganda Society*. An accomplished writer, Mathew has written for many leading publications, including *The Economist*, *Forbes*, *HBR*, *The Observer*, and *Ad Age*. *The Context Marketing Revolution* is his second book.

Mathew is a graduate of the University of Georgia and resident of Charleston, South Carolina. When he's not in the office you can find him at the local surf break in search of the perfect wave.